Contents

Acknowledgements

Contributing drivers:
Mario Hytten; Phil Andrews; Mark Bryan; David Hunt; Jari Nurminen; Emmanuele Naspetti; Allan McNish; Andy Wallace; Marco Apicella; Roger Orgee; Rod Birley; Gerry Taylor; Tony Trimmer.

General information and websites:
The Nostalgia forum at www.autosport.com; www.ten-tenths.com forums; www.tbk-lite.com forums; the old tbk.fameflame.dk forums; www.grandprixgames.com forums

Other contributors:
Stuart Knibbs – a big thank you to you for whetting my appetite about the Birmingham Superprix; Simon Lewis at www.simonlewis.com for his superb photographs; Ian Wagstaff for his pictures; Nick Bailey; David Lucas, Head of the Birmingham Road Race Department; The Birmingham Central Library (the Local Archives section); Many fans and marshals from the Nostalgia forum and Ten-Tenths forum; Stuart Dent – for his help and advice for contacting the right people; Kevin Wood from LAT Archives; Dominic Ostrowski from the BRSCC; Ben Laidlow, producer of the *Inside Out* programme by BBC West Midlands; Simon Edwards for various memorabilia; John Wisson for his marshal documents; Alastair Nash and Melanie Roberts for selling their collection of 1986-1990 *Motoring News* newspapers to me; The Communications Department of the Birmingham City Council; Simon Arron from *Motoring News*; Gregor Marshall for information about his father's involvement at the 1980 Lucas 'On The Streets' event; Rick Ashton from Ashton Plant Hire (Dudley) Ltd. for allowing me to look at the old Superprix Armco in its compound; *Birmingham Post & Mail* for its collection of old newspaper cuttings.

And finally, a huge thank you to my girlfriend, Sandra Burton, for supporting and putting up with me throughout this project. I am so grateful for your patience, and for giving me the motivation to complete the book.

David Page

Introduction

"The place is magic; better than Monaco" – not a description you would expect to hear of England's much derided second city, but Stefano Modena meant it. He was stepping from the cockpit of his Formula 3000 racer at the time: "Birmingham is something else; it is fantastic for the people of the city as well as for the people taking part. The circuit is not dangerous, as can be the case with street tracks – the drivers say it is bumpy, but then it's a street circuit so it would be bumpy, Birmingham is not an exception. I had no great problems with it, and in my opinion, Birmingham is a wonderful race."

That 'wonderful race' took place for five years, a half decade where the excitement and glamour of international motor racing came to the streets of the West Midlands. But those five years have now faded into obscurity. This is the story of how the races came about, and how they came to such a premature end. This is the story of the Superprix.

Superprix

The story of Birmingham's Motor Race

VELOCE

Other great books from Veloce Publishing –

www.veloce.co.uk

First published in November 2009 by Veloce Publishing Limited, 33 Trinity Street, Dorchester DT1 1TT, England. Fax 01305 268864/e-mail info@veloce.co.uk/web www.veloce.co.uk or www.velocebooks.com.
ISBN: 978-1-845842-42-0 UPC: 6-36847-04242-4

A road race for Birmingham?

The road to the Superprix was a long and winding one and began way back in the 1960s, just south of a town in France. "If one was to say, when was the seed sown? It was me standing at Le Mans in June 1961," claimed Birmingham City Councillor Peter Barwell.

A few years later, local man and sometime racing driver Martin Hone was having similar thoughts. In 1966, he opened the Opposite Lock Club; a heady mix of international jazz and motor racing. Hone's enthusiasm was infectious and it was noticed locally. A member of the City Council invited Hone to a meeting with various Councillors and others who were planning to move Birmingham forward: from its reputation as a drab, dark and run-down city, into a resurgent and exciting place to be – a seemingly impossible task. Hone's enthusiasm encouraged the Councillor to propose something quite revolutionary, something that would frighten other Council members; "a city internationally famous for the manufacture of cars, but with not many 'firsts' to our name, how about I organise the first ever street race in Britain?"

This was a task that faced many obstacles, one of which stood out above all, and Hone knew it; a British law that banned cars from exceeding the speed limit on public roads, even if they were closed. To get around this he would need a bill passed, and that would mean convincing Birmingham City Council, West Midlands County Council and Parliament itself. It would be an obstacle that stood in his way for twenty years to come. The law in question was only established in 1960, but it meant that motor racing or speed trials were prohibited on any public highway.

Over the years that followed, there were many meetings behind the scenes, and it was becoming clear that talk of a road race was not a popular issue amongst the city's aldermen and it lacked all party political support. Things looked bleak, but Hone refused to give in. He continued to lobby in the motorsport community and gained prominent supporters, such as Sir Stirling Moss, Graham Hill and Jackie Stewart.

Hone also garnered support from some political pockets in the Birmingham City Council. There came a much needed boost when the Chairman of the so-called Entertainment Sub-Committee of the Council's General Purpose Committee, Councillor John Silk, thought up a theme for a festival that would occur in the autumn of 1970. Martin Hone had an idea to boost his campaign for a road race by proposing a motoring pageant. The Committee then approached Hone, asking him to advise and assist in the running of the first ever Birmingham Motoring Festival, as Festival Liaison Officer. It was a perfect opportunity for Hone to see how much attention it would attract.

The Festival ran for fourteen days, opening on 24th August with a Vintage and Veteran Car Run. This was followed by a cavalcade of various cars, on a 2.1 mile circuit around the city centre streets, using a different theme each day. The roads would be closed from 11am to 3pm ever day, with tens of thousands of spectators gathering. Hone also linked the Festival with some midnight film matinees, black-tie dinners and balls, as well as some charity events.

A parade of Grand Prix racing brought the festival to a close, led by one of Martin Hone's supporters for a road race, Stirling Moss, in a Lotus 18. A ball attended by

Victor Turton, Lord Mayor Neville Bosworth and some of the famous drivers of the day concluded the evening. The Festival was hailed as a great success and attracted many visitors. The dream shared by so many people, especially Peter Barwell and Martin Hone, of the first ever road race on mainland Britain, was surely on the way to becoming a reality.

Following the success of the event, the possibility of an actual race was discussed between Martin Hone and Peter Barwell at some length. There was, perhaps, something of a private vendetta over who first had the idea of a Birmingham road race, and it is hard to tell, but, on the face of it, this hardly mattered one jot; the important thing was that everyone seemed very much in favour, particularly Councillor John Silk.

In January 1971, Barwell wrote to Silk, who was then Chairman of the Entertainment Sub-Committee, to put the proposal of a road race on a formal basis. As a result, it was raised at the General Purposes Committee on 12th March 1971. That was the first mention of a road race in the Council minutes. It was a fairly routine discussion, along the lines of 'let's consider a road race in Birmingham.' In April, Barwell received a letter from the Town Clerk stating that the proposal had been considered, and that further consideration was to be given to the possibilities of securing powers to hold an annual motor race. It was suggested that it would be on one of the carriageways of the Inner Ring Road.

Meanwhile, Hone, with all of his usual enthusiastic manner, threw himself at the project. He sounded out the feelings of the local aldermen, consulted with the police and the RAC, and then went specially to the Spanish Grand Prix, at Montjuich Park in Barcelona, to see just how things were done there. He compiled a dossier of photographs and, on his return, presented a white paper, titled 'Proposed Major Tourist Attraction for Birmingham City Centre devised by Martin Hone,' as advised by Birmingham City Council. Like any good proposal it delved deeply into the logistics and benefits, citing the value as a tourist attraction, publicity draw and business expander, and laid out his proposed route.

However, when the white paper was presented to the General Purposes Committee it caused uproar as, although many Council members were in favour of the proposal to promote the city, there were some people who thought the proposal was crazy and impossible and were decidedly against it. The main opposition of the Councillors was on the grounds that colossal expense would be incurred in staging such an event. Presenting a bill to Parliament in itself is very costly and many argued that the money would be better spent elsewhere. In particular, the then chief constable of Birmingham, Sir Derek Capper, bitterly opposed the proposed road race from a safety point of view. In fact, he was so against it that he was quoted as saying: "Over my dead body will it happen." Sir Derek died before the road race finally went ahead.

In May 1971, Councillor Victor Turton helped the road race campaign around the city's Inner Ring Road by announcing that he would make it the major project for his coming term as Lord Mayor. "I believe that motor racing in the centre of Birmingham would be a terrific tourist attraction to the city when linked up with other projects we have in mind," he explained as he fiercely promoted the scheme, and, eventually, a working party was set up to investigate the idea. The working party was duly formed and included: Basil Tye, RAC's Deputy Director; Geoff May, a former Secretary of the Porsche Club of Great Britain; Brian Fox and Roy Mitton, both leading members of the BRSCC Midland Centre that organised races at Mallory Park (the Birmingham City Council sponsored a race meeting at Mallory Park in 1970); Mike Broad, a local travel agent and Press Officer of the Association of West Midlands Motor Clubs; and Norman Austin, Area Manager of the RAC. The newly formed working party requested positive facts on the costs of hosting a road race, as well as on the faceless men who, reportedly, were prepared to finance the project. But politics and the petty disputes that eventually killed the event were already rearing their heads. The formation of Turton's working party was met with a blunt response from Silk, who commented "If this is going to happen, it's going to happen through the city and its proper channels with or without the assistance of other people." He clearly felt that the race should be the responsibility of the Sub-Committee, not of other self-appointed bodies.

Meanwhile, the concept itself was attacked by some politicians, notably from James Tye, Director General of the British Safety Council, who reportedly said that the whole plan was "a hare-brained scheme" and, even according to Tye, he mentioned that Jackie Stewart would have regarded it as a "comic proposal." A day earlier, Tye had travelled from London and been on a tour of the proposed racing circuit, around Birmingham's Inner Ring Road, and met a few officials from the City Council – some who were against the road race idea due to safety grounds.

Hone was still in action, too, and put together a business consortium that would offer to guarantee that the event would not cost the city a penny. It was estimated that it would cost £125,000 to set up the circuit, and that the grand total for all expenditure would be something like £300,000. A test day was even mooted with some well trusted local racers such as John Fitzpatrick with the Broadspeed Escort, Sid Taylor with

the CanAm McLaren and Alan Rollinson in the F5000 Surtees. Birmingham Corporation would have its roads closed for some periodic anti-skid tests, creating a good opportunity to show those involved how the affair should be set up. The plans for the test day were going smoothly, until a stumbling block came when a meeting of the Public Works Committee on 17th June, under the Chairmanship of Councillor Harold Edwards, turned down the idea. Edwards later explained: "It seemed that we don't have the legal power to lift the 30mph speed limit on these roads. Had we done so, we would have been accessories before the fact and liable to prosecution."

One could but hope that the various political infighting had reached a peaceful settlement by the time the race looked like a reality, and Councillor Silk envisaged a date in 1973. Hone reckoned things could be pushed through in time for 1972, a year earlier. However, Silk's Sub-Committee was to slow things rather: "To do it (a road race) in Birmingham we should have to promote a Private Parliamentary Bill," and this would cost anything from £5,000 upwards. "The Entertainments Sub-Committee has decided not to recommend the promotion of a bill until we have examined the idea more fully to see if it is worthwhile," Silk explained.

During November, Lord Mayor Turton was determined to see his plan work and argued it would boost passenger figures at Birmingham Airport and the Government's approval for the National Exhibition Centre would give extra impetus for the road race idea. Also, during the build-up towards Christmas 1971, Martin Hone announced there were eight companies bidding to sponsor the proposed road race in Birmingham, and claimed that an international company made a bid of £150,000 – which would be about £1.5 million in today's money.

Graham Hill commented: "It is an excellent scheme. It could be most interesting and bring a lot of benefit to motor racing and Birmingham. I would very much like to compete here but it depends how long the scheme takes."

In 1972 it was becoming apparent that the proposed road race was not gaining support from leading members of both parties on the City Council, some now convinced the plan to have a road race on the Inner Ring Road is a non-starter. Turton was hoping to avert this after the members were shaken by an official report on the likely costs of safety precautions and barriers. Also, they feared that a Ring Road bridge could be put out of action by a crashing racing car, to which Turton responded "a 10-ton lorry would do far more damage than a half-ton car if it hit a barrier!" On 28th April, he opened a display at Hangar Motors, Broad Street, which included a working scale model of the proposed Birmingham motor racing circuit.

The Birmingham International Motoring Festival ran again and, as before, a popular cavalcade of racing cars took place with drivers such as Stirling Moss, Gerry Birrell, Tom Wheatcroft, Andy Rouse and many other British drivers. Gerry Taylor took part in the festival with his Swish Anglia car to represent the saloon cars; "I remember we started in Victoria Square, down New Street, into Corporation Street left into Bull Street and left into Colmore Row and back to Victoria Square. Thousands lined the streets; the sound was raucous, and exciting. We had all manners of racing cars; I remember Derek Bell and Stirling Moss were there. I remember it vividly as I did the commentary for BBC Radio Birmingham (now Radio WM) along with Steve Roper. My mechanic, Dave Neal, took the car round the circuit."

It seemed like Hone had upped the ante with a proposed 1974 race, involving GT sports car and saloon races, followed with a possible F2 race. Now, he was pushing for a Grand Prix, but there were still many obstacles to overcome first, especially promotion for a bill that would be presented before Parliament in November. Its passage wouldn't be a smooth one, with objections likely from some MPs, and the whole bill could be lost in the corridors of power. In the meantime, the *Birmingham Evening Mail* ran a competition to find the best title to give the proposed race. The prize of £5 was won by a Mr D Ashton of Sparkhill, Birmingham with the suggestion; 'Festival Grand Circuit.' Luckily, it didn't stick.

It seemed impossible to deter Hone as the more obstacles were thrown in his path, the more vigour he attacked them with, but, again, politics became an issue. In 1974, a change of government came and Birmingham acquired a new tier of administration; a County Council. One of the members of the new body was a supporter of the road race idea, Kenneth Hardeman, who put a motion to the City Council to set up a committee and consider the implications of a road race in the city centre. He described the result: "Sadly, it became political. I was then a member of the Liberal minority party and, when I arranged for documents to be circulated to each member for the council meeting, there was violent objection from members of the two major opposition parties; on the grounds that I was wasting the Council's time in preparing documents, and, who was I to come up with ideas for motor races anyway."

Hone and Stirling Moss witnessed this political argument from the public gallery of the Council Chamber. The proposal was referred to the General Advisory Committee for full and detailed reports on the legal implications and requirements. Eventually, after much debate, the idea for a road race around the city gained all-party support.

However, it would cost a lot more than the original scheme from two years earlier. The cost of hosting a road race in Birmingham would have gone up to £30,000, as was estimated by the Martin Hone-Sir Stirling Moss consortium. It was hoped that a Formula 5000 would be the main event of the road race, with support racing from historic sports cars, followed by a stream of British Leyland models used as transport for the famous drivers attending. The third event would be a race for smaller formula cars, followed by vintage cars and possibly a production car race for Midlands products. The drivers would practice on a Sunday, with the races on the following Monday.

Then in October, the City Council voted in favour of the promotion of the new legislation by 65 votes to 29. It was a crucial move and the momentum was kept going with The Motoring Festival and the Vintage and Veteran Car Run that would be arranged in 1975.

In September, West Midlands County Council suggested that Parliament should be approached in order to obtain wide-ranging powers that would enable a road race to take place through the city centre of Birmingham. A proposal had to be put before Parliament by November to create a Birmingham road race for 1976.

At the end of 1974, a draft West Midlands County Council bill was drawn up and it secured the necessary majority to take it to Parliament. It gained support from all parties as the City Council voted in favour of the promotion of the new legislation by 65 votes to 29.

'Practical difficulties' had been foreseen by the Chief Constable, the Chief Fire Officer and the County Surveyor but, fortunately, there was enough support from enthusiastic Council members.

In early 1975, the Parliamentary bill was drafted with the relevant clauses and the talk of a race in 1976 was back on.

Martin Hone now knew the crowds it was possible to attract to the motoring festivals in the city centre. Previous events proved a good indicator of its popularity and, in 1975, the Duckhams Motoring Festivals attracted many motor racing stars. Hone had been keen to see that The Vintage and Veteran Car Run, from Stratford to Birmingham, becomes the 'Midland' equivalent of the London to Brighton run. It had become a successful event, Hone recalls: "We were getting a terrific turnout. 70,000 spectators were stretched from Stratford to Birmingham watching it."

However, in 1976 the General Purposes Committee, of which Marjorie Brown was Chairman, cancelled both events for the year. This didn't deter the push for the road race bill to go to Parliament, although the bill contained a clause concerning municipal trading and was subsequently thrown out in the House of Commons. So, unfortunately, the road race further down the bill did not even get a hearing.

The National Exhibition Centre was opened in 1976 and it was hoped that the International Motor Show would be hosted there, alternating with London Earls Court in 1978. It showed that there was plenty of interest in the automobile and motorsport industry.

Martin Hone said: "My aim was to create a tourist enterprise and it turned out to be a motor race. I wanted it under way to coincide with the opening of the National Exhibition Centre, but the political infighting put paid to that ... I want a motoring festival, the motor show and a race which will turn the world spotlight on Birmingham. It could do the same for Birmingham as it has for Monte Carlo."

Top and bottom: The 1975 Duckhams parade on New Street. (Ian Bower)

The first day of February, on a quiet Sunday morning, the silence was shattered by a flat V12 engine going around Smallbrook Ringway and St Martin's Circus; part of the proposed circuit.

Martin Hone invited the Brabham Formula One team to bring its Alfa Romeo-powered BT45 car to be driven around the circuit by Patrick Neve. It was a publicity stunt, and also to make a film, which would be shown on the BBC's 'Nationwide' programme later on that week.

It was the first time a racing car had been allowed on the roads of the proposed circuit – if it ever became a reality. For the residents of the tower blocks nearby, overlooking the road, it was an abrupt end to their Sunday morning lie-in.

The Brabham's progress around the roads took place in short bursts, even on a cold Sunday morning – completely closing this small section of the Ringway would have disrupted 30 bus routes and three train departures from the New Street train station.

The City Council and police enforced that the car should only run for 10 minute periods, between the arrivals and departures of the trains and buses. They warned that the car should not exceed the speed limit. These restrictions did not make the BBC's job easier, but it used a television trick by 'under-cranking' so the car would appear to be going very fast on the screen.

The restrictions also caused problems for Patrick Neve, who only the week before had driven in the Brazilian Grand Prix at Interlagos. The car would not go at 30mph, and he touched 90mph around the proposed circuit. The whole event was supervised by Assistant Chief Constable William Donaldson, and he turned a blind eye to the speeding Brabham.

Brian Thomas, a resident on the 27th floor of nearby Sentinel Towers, found it difficult to turn a deaf ear and stormed down to complain. He argued the pros and cons of a possible Grand Prix with Martin Hone, who said that the noise coming from the Alfa Romeo engine was music to his ears and he stoutly refused to cover his ears like everyone else at the occasion.

Home said: "After nearly seven years we're still going forward. Everyone, especially the police, have been very cooperative and it all went off very well."

Environmental Health Officers were at the demo run and took sound readings which reached 129 decibels. They estimated that more than one car would give 135 decibels; regarded as a hazard. The impressive noise was heard a quarter of a mile away!

The road race project suffered another blow in March when Sir Stanley Yapp, the influential leader of the City Council, withdrew his support. It was a move that could have considerable impact on the future of the project. In the following month, the City Council put forward another proposal to promote a Private Bill in Parliament. Again, it was defeated, by 10 votes. 51 Councillors voted for the project, with 61 Councillors voting against it. Stirling Moss was "bitterly disappointed," but Martin Hone was still determined not to give up: "I swear that one day there will be motor racing on the streets of Birmingham. Someone will have the courage to do it."

Birmingham hosted the 1978 International Motor Show at the newly opened National Exhibition Centre, and Hone grabbed the opportunity to promote the event by gaining permission from the City Council for his company, International Festival Services, to run the 'On The Streets' spectacular, which took part on Sunday 8th October. He said the police gave him special permission for the cars to be driven above the 30mph limit at 'demonstration' speed. Hone would not state how fast the cars would go, but ensured that the crowd would be entertained by the speed and sounds from the cars.

The event was sponsored by Bristol Street Motors and P J Evans. Many famous drivers attended the event such as; Sir Jack Brabham, Juan Manuel Fangio, Dan Gurney, Carroll Shelby, Roy Salvadori, Tony Brooks, Sir Stirling Moss and even a young Nigel Mansell.

The motoring cavalcade covered a mile and a half circuit consisting of Hurst Street, Moat Lane and Barford Street, which surrounded the wholesale market. The start and finish was at Moat Lane, near the Bull Ring. The cars invited to the cavalcade ran in groups, completing ten laps of the circuit for three hours. Barricades were erected to ensure the safety of the viewing public.

Between 100,000 and 122,000 spectators turned out to see 120 racing cars demonstrating. Also, it attracted much interest and support from the City Council, with then Lord Mayor Ted Hanson and many Councillors, including Barwell, giving their support.

Roy Salvadori described the 'On The Streets' spectacular as "one of most exciting weekends of my life." It was a big compliment, considering the glamour and excitement he had experienced in his racing career.

There was plenty of burnt rubber and screaming from different engines that rang out in the city centre. Monaco didn't seem so far away. Unfortunately, at one point during the event, three spectators were injured when a Formula Three driver, Paul Morton, crashed out of control because his rear brakes failed in his car.

A few days later, legal experts debated whether or not Morton could face a road traffic charge. The police also launched an inquiry to determine if an offence had been committed, but a spokesman said the cars were not ordinary road vehicles. A mother of two, Eleanor Roberts, claimed compensation from Birmingham City Council for leg and foot injuries, which kept her off work for two weeks.

A spokesman for the Council said that insurance cover had been extended to cover spectator injury during the event, and Mrs Croft's claim would be processed. The accident emphasised the possible dangers of the sport to onlookers, as well as to the drivers.

With the popularity of the parade and the relaxed atmosphere during it, the biggest scenario the police had to deal with was clearing the rooftops from buildings surrounding St Martin's church, where people found useful vantage points from which to watch the cars!

Paving the way towards a street race

Despite the troubles encountered at the first 'On The Streets' event, a second was organised in 1980. The 'Lucas On The Streets Sport Spectacular' was run over a 2.5 mile circuit around the back streets of Hurst Street, Moat Lane and Barford Street, by the wholesale markets which were used as a paddock for the racing cars. The temporary circuit had a racing feel as it was fully decorated with racing banners, and marshaled by members of the British Motor Racing Marshal's Club. Again, many famous names, associated with well-known cars, took part.

There were seven Formula One World Champions at the event, and guests were given the chance to run solo around the demonstration circuit: Juan Manuel Fangio in his Mercedes 300 SLR (which he drove to second place on the 1955 Mille Miglia); Sir Jack Brabham in his loaned Brabham BT2 Formula 2 car; Carroll Shelby and Roy Salvadori, reunited with their 1959 Le Mans-winning Aston Martin DBR1 car; Phil Hill guesting in a JCB Ferrari Dino; and the newly crowned 1980 Formula One World Champion, Alan Jones, in his Saudia-Leyland-sponsored Williams FW07B.

Prompted by the success of the event, and questions over the Birmingham road race project, Barwell said publicly: "I think the time is right following the tremendous success ... to reopen the issue." City engineers had already made a feasibility study of the proposed circuit drawn up by Martin Hone. They found no major snags with the plans. The two mile circuit met international regulations and a major international race

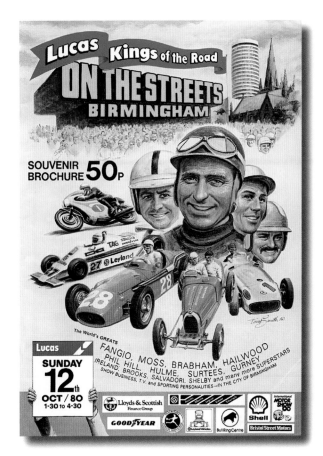

1980 'On The Streets' programme.

could be staged as early as 1984, followed by more prestigious events afterwards.

Roughly a year later, Hone and council leaders felt they had finally found a suitable circuit to host a road race in Birmingham. In October, Martin Hone submitted a package of proposals to the City Council, believing he had found a 2.5 mile route around the city that would fit the bill.

This came after scrapping a controversial proposal to run the circuit through Lee Bank council housing estate. The circuit was extremely cramped and far too tight to race there, plus, it would invoke many complaints from residents of the estate regarding disruption and noise. Local Labour representative Councillor Albert Bore discovered the leaked Lee Bank proposal after a private meeting with council officers and Martin Hone. "I am appalled that such an idea should even be discussed," said Bore. "A motor race through Lee Bank would be totally disruptive for people living there."

Grandstanding would have to be provided and roads would require widening in places. The suggested layout would cause a lot of problems with diverting the traffic, but Councillor Bore said: "The officers should not be wasting their time discussing a scheme as ridiculous as this." However, the emergency services were happier with Hone's proposal, compared with the '71 proposals, Lee Bank having better access for fire engines and ambulances. Assistant Chief Constable Ken Evans said of Hone: "There may be disadvantages to this route, but I am sure he is the right chap to get this thing off the ground."

Eventually, in the summer, the Lee Bank circuit was scrapped, together with the original, 1971 route around the city centre. A new proposal was needed before the project could progress.

The Chairman of the city's General Purposes Committee, Councillor Bernard Zissman, who was chairing a working party investigating the road race scheme, said they had asked a small group to find a route, and report within a month or six weeks. The *Birmingham Post* quoted him on 23rd October: "We have overcome the objections in principle. We think that all the problems can be resolved if we can get a route that will satisfy statutory bodies and will be satisfactory to residents."

Hone would not reveal the new route to the media until Councillor Zissman inspected it the following week. It is claimed the drawings were still submitted to the West Midlands County Highways Department and police for approval. Martin Hone and the City Council had been hoping to stage motor racing in time for the next year's Rotary International Conference in Birmingham, but it now appeared that 1985 would be a realistic date to aim for.

John Richardson, the Divisional Engineer, was given the responsibility of creating the Superprix and the area where it would be based. It could have been nearer the city centre, based on Queensway or around Five Ways, or on different roads around Bristol Street, but these were all rejected for safety or convenience reasons.

The City Council was sticking to its original objectives for hosting a road race in the streets of Birmingham, as it had always wanted to stage a major tourist attraction that would show Birmingham in its best light, convinced that the new route would provide the best background possible for satellite television cameras.

Then, finally, on 7th September came a newly-proposed 2.5 mile circuit for the Birmingham Grand Prix, which meant racing cars could be zooming around in two years' time. Martin Hone wanted to bring some publicity to the new route. To do this, the City Council and Hone suggested a big, revived 'On The Streets' motoring spectacular around the circuit for October, as a dummy run and curtain raiser for the 1984 International Motor Show at the National Exhibition Centre in Birmingham. He claimed that he had been working on the newly-proposed route for three years.

The circuit had been designed to go the wrong way round the one-way road system to prevent the public trying out the 2.5 mile race route.

It was proposed that the new circuit would stage racing over a Bank Holiday, with practising on the Sunday and the main event on the Monday. This would keep the upheaval caused to everyday traffic and bus services to a minimum, but would also mean maximum attraction as an international spectacle to the world.

1984 proved to be a very important year for Martin Hone and the prime movers of the Birmingham Road Race Bill. It was brought up once more, before the General Purposes Committee. The city solicitors agreed that a redrafted bill should be prepared, and the council employed Hone's company, International Festival Services, as a consultant to help pass the bill through Parliament.

This time, a suitable circuit layout was needed and Martin Hone had already revealed his plans of the Birmingham Superprix layout back in September 1983. Hone claimed that it took him three years to design the layout. "I know circuits inside out, I know what the drivers want, I know what the spectators need, I know where the sponsor banners go because I have done it all my life," Hone explained.

He added that he remembers taking Councillor Marjorie Brown, Councillor Barwell, the City Engineer and the Chief of Police around the circuit in his motor home. The police, fire brigade and ambulance officials agreed that the newly proposed circuit would cause the least disruption of through traffic and local traffic and, more importantly, would be close enough to emergency services in the event of an accident. Martin Hone created a unique priority corridor leading from the circuit to the Birmingham Accident Hospital, only half a mile away.

The proposed road race still brought criticism, and Councillor Clive Wilkinson (Labour Soho) said claims that the road race would bring about £11 million of trade

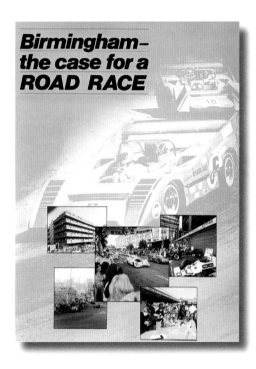

1984 BSP Council promotion pack.

and income for the city, as well as a total of 250,000 visitors, were exaggerated. Although, Councillor Neville Bosworth (Conservative Edgbaston) said that the Council remained tremendously interested in the plans and was still willing to promote the bill.

The Council was still seeking support from the local residents and businesses in the Bristol Street/Belgrave Middleway area, so it set up a postal referendum for 4520 people to vote 'yes' or 'no' for the road race plan at the start of May.

The City Council organised, and put together, a delegation to go to the 1984 Monaco Grand Prix, to prepare for staging a similar event in the city. But it wasn't well prepared, and upon discovering the hotels in Monaco were fully booked the delegation had to stay in nearby Nice! John Charlton, a member of the delegation, was "amazed to see that the racing circuit could be opened up for the use of ordinary traffic after only 21 minutes." The delegation agreed: "We think Birmingham can do it better." Charlton also added: "We are absolutely convinced that the facilities we can offer for a race in Birmingham are considerably better than you can get in Monte Carlo."

Four weeks later, after the start of the postal referendum, it came to a conclusion; it was very good news, showing a four-to-one in favour by residents and businesses to stage international motor racing in the streets of Birmingham. It was revealed that 1270 people were in favour and 283 people against the proposed plans.

On Sunday 15th July, in the early hours of the morning, a 3-litre Cosworth-powered GRID car driven by Steve Thompson tested the proposed circuit, under the supervision of a police motorcycle and a close eye from Martin Hone. Occasionally, the police motorcyclist had to flag down the car in order to keep up with Thompson! It evoked many complaints about the noise from the local residents nearby.

Mark Ellis, a reporter from the *Birmingham Post*, gave readers a rare insight into the proposed street circuit when he sat in the passenger seat in a replica Ford GT40 car, with Mike Porter as the driver. The car reached speeds of 140mph along Belgrave Road Straight!

The same week, it was reported that Sir Philip Knights, the Chief Constable of the West Midlands, issued a strongly worded statement regarding the demonstration run. He considered whether or not drivers exceeding the speed limit around the proposed circuit should be prosecuted. According to Philip Knights, the promotional agreement was changed, as originally that one car had to travel around the circuit within the speed limit.

Three high performance cars led by a police motorcyclist then made three laps at high speed. The Chief Constable threatened to withdraw police support for events similar to this demonstration run. Hone explained shortly afterwards that he had made lengthy arrangements with the police and praised them for their help to make this happen.

Finally, on 14th October, the practicalities of staging a major motorsport event were tested in the 'On The Streets' motor cavalcade, and it was the best event that Martin Hone and his company had organised. It was sponsored by Davenport's, a local brewery best known for its home deliveries. The festival was called 'The Chequered Bitter Classic' after one of Davenport's brews. According to Hone, it cost £180,000 to stage the festival. Only £20,000 came from the City Council, the rest through private sponsorship.

It would be the 11th time that racing cars had been unleashed on Birmingham's streets, and the most important by far because it used the same 2.5 mile circuit as the one proposed to stage real motor racing on August Bank Holiday in 1986. Hone's ultimate aim was a Birmingham Grand Prix but he realised that this would have to be achieved in stages, starting with a race meeting for saloons and sports cars.

It was a feast for the eye and ear. An orgy of nostalgia for the 200,000 spectators that attended the Festival, which ran around the Birmingham Superprix proposed circuit – and all with a 40mph speed limit. The show continued until 5.30pm when the roads were re-opened to the general public.

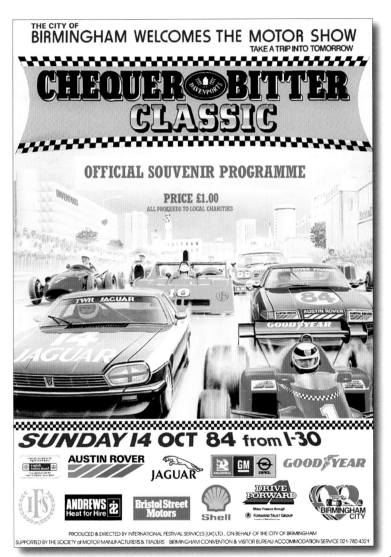

Chequer Bitter Classic programme.

"I can see Grand Prix racing on these streets. The number of people shows the support," claimed ex-Formula One driver John Watson.

It was a crowd puller, and the long-running saga of Birmingham's capabilities to be a motorsport venue of the future gained a massive vote of confidence from some of the great names of the sport. Now, the enthusiasm and overwhelming public support would be pressed home, and moves by Birmingham City Council to apply in November for Parliamentary permission to stage motor racing would be made in full. Also, it was a perfect dress rehearsal for the police and fire services to prepare for the real thing.

Organiser Martin Hone was jubilant: "It's the most fantastic day Birmingham has ever seen. We have been telling them for years that Birmingham should host Grand Prix racing; hopefully someone will now take notice."

Now, the fun was over and the serious political work still had to be done. Less than a month later, after a very successful motoring event, the Birmingham City Council approved taking the Birmingham Road Race Bill to Parliament; 90 Birmingham Councillors voting for the bill and 13 against it (with five absentees), on 6th November. The Road Race Bill was deposited to Parliament with high hopes.

The Lord Mayor of Birmingham, Councillor Reg Hales, presented the Road Race Bill to the House of Commons on Tuesday 27th November. He arrived at the Houses of Parliament in style, and whisked to the Commons in an Aston Martin racing car driven by Sir Stirling Moss. He said:

"The people of Birmingham want this race. The commercial sectors want it. The motor racing fraternity wants it. The City Council wants it. The County Council wants it. The economy of Birmingham and the West Midlands need it. Fun, international glamour, tourism, jobs. How can Parliament say no!"

Two days later, the Birmingham Road Race Bill went through to Parliament, despite opposition from Labour MPs, Jeff Rooker and Clare Short – the latter was to be a permanent thorn in the side of the race. Now, the finishing line was fast approaching for Martin Hone, Birmingham City Council and the people of Birmingham to make the Birmingham Superprix into reality.

After the crucial meetings at the Houses of Parliament, Bernie Ecclestone (President of the Formula One Constructors' Association) said: "I've no idea whether or not a Grand Prix could be held in Birmingham, but it would be nice to see it happen." Ecclestone's words gave hope and the mechanics of the project began to run smoother than before. However, the RAC Motor Sports Association (the sport's governing body in the UK) threatened to end the dream when it said it was "unlikely" to grant the

A Porsche 917K on the Chequer Bitter Classic.
(Jeremy Jackson)

A Brabham BT30 on the Chequer Bitter Classic.
(Jeremy Jackson)

City of Birmingham permission to hold a street race. The year ended with mixed hopes and fortunes for the those still wanting to see any form of racing in the streets of Birmingham.

1986 would bring some final arrangements before a race could be confirmed. The political stirrings in Birmingham were making the 10 permanent UK circuits (e.g. Silverstone, Donington, Brands Hatch etc.) worried that the possibility of street venues would detract from the permanent motorsport circuits. At the end of January, Silverstone Circuits Limited circulated a telex with a strong stance on the subject of street racing. It read: "Silverstone Circuits Limited has been asked by a number of newspapers/TV/radios for its attitude towards racing on the streets of British cities.

In coming out strongly against the principal [sic] of these events, Silverstone Circuits Limited made the following statement: 'Racing on the public highway is against the law. Therefore, to cater for the needs of races, permanent circuits had to be built by private investors – individuals and organisations alike. Over many years, they have ploughed their resources into purpose built circuits to cater for all the needs of the sport, from club race level through to Grand Prix. Additionally, the country's permanent circuits actively encourage all aspects of motor racing, helping the beginners, subsiding the enthusiasts' events and providing training grounds for drivers, officials, marshals, plus facilities for testing racing vehicles which would not be provided by temporary street circuits. The permanent circuits are

The famous Russell Brookes Andrews Heat for Hire Opel Manta 400 on the Chequer Bitter Classic.
(Jeremy Jackson)

19

able to provide the best, safest facilities for competitors and spectators alike. With two circuits in the country licensed to run Grand Prix and others catering for a wide cross section of events, we do not see the need for the law to be changed to permit street racing.'"

There was a great deal of pressure building up as the circuits registered their disapproval of the idea. The Birmingham City Council threatened to take the Royal Automobile Club to court if it stuck to its intended refusal to licence the proposed road race. So, the city councillors arranged a meeting with the Motor Sports Council in early February, and the matter was quickly resolved when the RAC gave Birmingham an ultimatum; it would drop the opposition if Parliament passed the bill to give the go-ahead to close the roads for racing.

That was one hurdle out of the way, although the City Council was also still trying to find a compromise with the RAC Motor Sport Association, which mentioned it may not issue a racing licence for national events in Birmingham. But, as before, if Parliament passed the bill then the RAC MSA would agree to grant the city a licence to host a racing event.

Behind the scenes at Birmingham City Council, there was much work to be done, such as consulting with the various transport, highways, gas, fire, water, police, and sewerage and health authorities. It was very time consuming but it needed to prove a workable plan to show to Parliament, to sway the votes and get the Road Race Bill approved. It was a PR exercise to generate support and get 100 MPs to back the bill. The City Council would continue to petition for the bill until 30th March, in the hope that the Birmingham Road Race Bill would be awarded Royal Assent in July. However, there was a blow as on the same day when the second reading of the Road Race Bill was blocked in the House

of Commons. It was believed that it was the same people that originally blocked the bill in November 1984 – there were still some obstacles to overcome.

Then a compromise over the objections to the Road Race Bill emerged. This involved the reduction of the number of days allowed for the erection and dismantling of the circuit and the provision of suitable compensation terms, to be arranged with the local traders, for loss of business caused by the event. The organisers tried hard to make residents living near the circuit happy and offered access to the event by giving out free passes. The city also offered to pay for the people living on or near the circuit to go away on race days if desired.

A Labour MP, Terry Davies, negotiated at that time; representing the group of MPs who were against the bill. Davies had always been against the road race because he doubted the event would make profit based on the scale that was forecast. He felt the figures presented were far too optimistic and that it was a risky move for the Council, which was confident it could make money from the event.

The promoters of the bill felt the event would make a profit, and amended the bill by adding a clause that if it did not make a profit after three years, they would stop it. Davies said that those opposing the bill didn't want to hold them to three years, and negotiated with the Council to amend the bill to state if the street race did not make a profit after five years, it would then be stopped.

It was a very crucial part of the Road Race Bill, known as the 'Sunset Clause.' The Road Race Committee kept its hopes up, and in February the RAC MSA indicated that it would grant Birmingham a race licence, provided the Road Race Bill was passed on 2nd April. The first day of April was a very crucial one for the

City of Birmingham as Members of Parliament voted on the Road Race Bill. The Commitee acknowledged that 100 votes were needed to support the Road Race Bill before the 10pm deadline. Eventually, in the second reading, 202 MPs voted for the bill and 68 MPs against it. Birmingham cleared the final hurdle the following day, and the finishing line was so near.

The Road Race Bill had two main aims:

Firstly, to create a major tourist attraction for Birmingham and the West Midlands with a race through the city streets on one day of the year, all preparation and practice runs happening on the day before. The race, which will have a saloon car focus, would take place through city streets which, due to a unique post-war road development, provide a natural urban road race circuit.

Secondly, to promote Birmingham as a motor city, thus, giving its industrial and business base in the West Midlands a much needed shot in the arm.

In order to meet the August deadline imposed by Parliament for the Road Race Bill to gain Royal Assent, the Road Race Committee had to work on designing the circuit and how it would fit into day-to-day life.

There were a lot of negotiations on how to put together the Road Race Bill to make it accessible for the people of Birmingham. The bill authorised the city to hold a motor race over only two days, a Sunday and Monday at the end of August, over the Bank Holiday weekend. The closure of certain roads was allowed over these two days from 9am to 6pm.

Permission was granted for such things as making of bylaws, finance arrangements such as borrowing, film and broadcasting rights, and levying of admission charges. The pit area and grandstands could be set up and Armco barriers could be erected. The period allowed for erecting and removing barriers was limited to ten days prior and five days after the event, to avoid disrupting the traffic around the circuit and access for nearby residents.

After the Road Race Bill was approved by Members of Parliament, the City Council stuck to its intentions of having a road race to show off the city as an attractive place in which to live and work and to encourage new businesses to come to Birmingham.

On 11th June, the same Labour MPs who opposed the Road Race Bill blocked its progress again in order to force a debate. Although the bill had passed its second reading, the opposition prevented it getting the nod and a full-scale discussion and vote by Members of Parliament was needed.

The opposition objected to the bill because MPs felt they should be given an opportunity to put forward some amendments and have a debate about it. However, it was unlikely it would jeopardise the approval of the road race.

After a few weeks of negotiations, the City Council and the opposition finally came to an agreement when the opposition group said that permission to spend taxpayers' money on the street racing event should be withdrawn if the race was not making a profit by 1991. The clause was thrown out by 127 votes to 20, but Sir Reginald Eyre promised that an amendment to meet this point would be added to the bill.

In July, it was expected that the bill would get an unopposed third reading in the following few weeks, getting to the House of Lords before the summer recess.

Birmingham City Council proposed to form a seven-strong motor race unit to organise and plan to bring international motoring racing to the streets the next August Bank Holiday. The new unit consisted of a team of employees within the Chief Executive's department, and would be run by two existing senior officers acting as Controller and Deputy. Five additional posts, headed by a full-time project officer, were being recruited at an expected total of nearly £50,000 a year. David Lucas, an RAC regional committee member, was appointed head of the new road race unit in mid-September. Now the City Council wanted to see things happening with the sponsorship to help it finance the road race.

However, there were some ugly scenes away from the public eye because Martin Hone, since November 1984, had produced an important document from previous council incumbents saying that, if he ever got this through Parliament, his would be the company and he the man to run the event for the City of Birmingham. He was summoned to the City Administrator's office and told the city would like to put together a tender for him. Martin Hone protested on the basis of having this crucial document that allowed him to run the whole event.

The problem was that the Labour Party won control of the City of Birmingham in May, and it didn't recognise any agreements made by previous incumbents. Hone acknowledged that he found himself bidding for his own idea, with no clue as to who else was involved. He was informed only that there were other parties interested and making bids.

Martin Hone's company and others also interested were invited to submit a sponsorship proposal to the city. Martin Hone remembers making his presentation: "I went to the City Council House, in front of a board of 30 people including; city leaders, solicitors, the Lord Mayor, Councillors and all the people that we had been working with for years, and with whom we had built up a good relationship. I guaranteed them they'd make a profit because I had already got my agreements in place for television and sponsorship, and with Bernard

Ecclestone for FIA Formula 3000, and I knew I didn't need a solitary person through the pay-gate to make a profit. I gave them a guaranteed sum in writing; I made a 45 minute presentation with pictures and movies."

Afterwards, he waited for the verdict. Other bidders walked in, one of whom was Andrew Marriott of CSS Promotions; a well-established motorsport marketing company based in London, also responsible for the commercial backing of the city's bid for the 1992 Olympics.

When Andrew Marriott emerged after less than 10 minutes into his presentation, Martin Hone knew his local bid was lost:

"It was like a knife going into my gut and out the other side."

The contract was awarded to CSS Promotions for organising sponsorships. The Council's decision caused controversy. People had to defend themselves, such as Mr Denis Howell (Labour MP for Small Heath), a consultant to CSS Promotions and president of Birmingham's Olympic Committee. Howell said that he had no connections with its commercial work for the race, nor with its commercial backing for the city's Olympics bid, he simply helped the Road Race Bill get through Parliament.

In early discussions about a Birmingham street race, there was optimistic talk of a Grand Prix, and the name 'Festival Grand Circuit' was suggested in July 1972 by a Mr D Ashton of Sparkhill, Birmingham.

It was another thirteen years – in October 1985 – before the Road Race Committee gave the event a name. By that time, it was accepted that the event was not going to be a Formula One race, and so could not be called a Grand Prix. The Commitee came up with the name 'The Birmingham Superprix.'

Amongst the controversy over Martin Hone and the City Council, the Commitee pulled off a coup as, six weeks after giving CSS Promotions the contract, it acquired title sponsorship from car parts and bicycle firm Halfords. The Redditch-based firm would become the main sponsor, paying £70,000 to Birmingham City Council.

The new sponsorship terms of the Birmingham Superprix meant that Halfords had the rights for the circuit corners. It chose to name the roundabout at the top of the Belgrave Middleway 'Halfords Corner,' as this was the part of the circuit it thought would get most publicity – a wide hairpin corner, making it the slowest on the track, with the best vantage point, which should attract large numbers of spectators. It hoped that 'Halfords Corner' would become a well-known Birmingham landmark, and not just a roundabout associated with an annual two- or three-day event.

Gallaher Tobacco offered a sponsorship deal but Birmingham City Council turned it down. The Council took a big risk in banning tobacco advertisements on the racing cars, or on advertising hoardings scattered around the street circuit, as it did on its city buses, but wanted to send out a health-conscious message from the start.

Finally, at the end of October, the Road Race Bill was given Royal Assent and renamed the 'Birmingham City Council Act 1985.' The dream of having a road race in the streets of Birmingham had been fulfilled. The city was now set to be the first ever British municipality to host a road race in mainland Great Britain.

For the handful of early dreamers, especially Peter Barwell and many other Councillors, all the work had been worthwhile. Sir Reginald Eyre, promoter of the Birmingham City Council Act, said to the *Birmingham Mail* on 30th October: "This marks yet another milestone in Birmingham's drive to bring new ideas and attractions to the city.

"The motor racing is a colourful and exciting idea which, with associated entertainments, will mean a good family day out in the city centre."

Soon after the Royal Assent was given, a leaflet about everything the Council was doing, including staging the road race which it promised would not cost the taxpayer a penny, was distributed to every household in Birmingham.

In a referendum, 93 per cent of people living in the area voted in favour of the Superprix and for the race to take place there.

As the year came to a near close, Birmingham City Council pulled off a big motorsport coup by announcing, on 17th December, that it had won an official sanction to host a Formula 3000 European Championship event in its programme, for the first weekend of the August Bank Holiday in 1986.

1986 – The final preparations

Echoing Bernie Ecclestone's words about Birmingham hosting a Grand Prix in the future, the city could not hope to secure full-blown Formula One racing in its streets because, for some years, the racing calendar was committed so far ahead and any circuit had to be tried and tested for at least two years.

Bringing racing to the streets of Birmingham came at a price, as the City Council paid £100,000 to secure the 26 teams of the F3000 series. John Webb was a strong supporter of the Thundersports series and wanted this to be the bill-topper for the inaugural race, although his suggestion was met with little approval as the race organisers were geared towards open wheelers.

Councillor Mrs Marjorie Brown, Chairman of the city's Road Race Committee, announced the decision to bring the teams to Birmingham by unveiling the first section of Armco barrier at the side of the road racetrack at the Highgate Island (which would become the Halfords Corner), together with racing driver Tony Trimmer. She hailed this as another major first for the city.

Behind the scenes, there were some warring words as the City Council had sponsorship problems, with the headline in the local press dated on 1st June: 'AUSTIN PRIX NON-STARTER.'

It reported that Austin Rover, Birmingham's biggest employer, claimed the company which had given Birmingham the name 'Motor City' had been shut out of the round-the-streets event because the councillors' demands were too high.

A spokesman for the car manufacturer was quoted as saying that its joint sponsorship deal had been rejected, and instead they had been offered the chance of providing 12 Metro cars for a possible celebrity event. The company refused, claiming the deal would cost almost as much as the entire day event, but it was keen to be involved in the race. Austin Rover accused the City Councillors of making it impossible for it. Councillor John Charlton, member of the Road Race Committee, said many attempts had been made to contact Austin Rover's Chairman, Harold Musgrave, without any success. Also, he claimed that the firm did express interest but couldn't confirm any commitment of support.

Instead, the Council arranged for Renault 5 turbo cars to be provided by the French car manufacturer, to race five laps of the Superprix circuit in the celebrity event.

The Birmingham Superprix circuit was summoned to a track inspection by the RAC MSA just before Christmas. It revealed that there was insufficient run-off area at four specific parts of the circuit, and the calculated average lap speed caused some concern.

On Monday 17th March 1986, John Webb and his company, Motor Circuit Developments, which controlled other British circuits such as Brands Hatch, Oulton Park and Snetterton, signed an exclusive three year contract with Birmingham City Council to help stage the Birmingham Superprix. Webb, widely regarded as 'Mr Motor Racing' in Britain, had proved that big business and motor racing mix, attracting an increasing amount of business sponsorship to the sport and to the City of Birmingham. In addittion, he stated that his company "will advertise and offer guidance to the Council in all matters concerning or affecting motor racing."

Mrs Marjorie Brown, Chairman of the Road Race Sub-Committee was quoted: "It is this professionalism and expertise in motor racing that the City of Birmingham wanted to ensure the best possible team was organising our first racing on the streets."

On signing his contract with the City Council, Webb said: "Normally, a circuit has to start with an amateur meeting – Birmingham has gone ten times better. It has started off with the most professional team it is possible to assemble in this country."

The City Council issued a press release on the same day, revealing the race programme for the 24th and 25th August. The timetable would look like this:

Sunday 24th August 1986		
0900-0945	F3000	Untimed Group A practice session
1000-1045	F3000	Untimed Group B practice session
1100-1140	Thundersports	Heat 1 qualifying session
1200-1240	Thundersports	Heat 2 qualifying session
1300-1345	F3000	Group A first qualifying session
1400-1445	F3000	Group B first qualifying session
1500-1530	F3000	Group A second qualifying session
1545-1615	F3000	Group B second qualifying session
1645 Race 1	Thundersports	Heat 1: 10 laps
1715 Race 2	Thundersports	Heat 2: 10 laps

Monday 25th August 1986		
0900-0940	Pro-Am Renault	Untimed practice session
1000-1020	F3000	Warm-up
1035-1100	FF1600	Untimed practice session
1100	F3000 drivers' briefing	
1120-1155	Formula Libre	Untimed practice session
1215 Race 3	Pro-Am Renault	2x 5 laps
1300 Race 4	Thundersports	Trophy Race: 30 laps
1400	F3000 pit lane open	
1420	Countdown to the F3000 race	
1435 Race 5	The Halfords Birmingham Superprix	52 laps
1635 Race 6	FF1600	10 laps
1715 Race 7	Formula Libre	15 laps

After losing out for his own bid to CSS Promotions, the Council offered Martin Hone £70,000 to organise a repeat of the 1984 Chequered Bitter run – with cars and champions at all expenses covered. However, that event had cost Hone £166,000 and he reveals "I pared it down and down, but couldn't get it under £110,000. I wasn't prepared to lower my standards, so I declined their offer, whereupon they issued a press release to the tune: 'Martin Hone turns down £70,000 cash offer to run parades.'"

The media gave it enormous coverage in April, that continued on and off for some time. There were other newspaper headlines which included: 'ROAD RACE PLAN ROCKED BY ROW OVER CONTRACTS,' 'ROAD RACE DREAM THAT IS NOW A NIGHTMARE,' and 'ROAD RACE GAG ON HONE IS DENIED.'

The last headline refers to the contract that the City Council offered to Martin Hone. He referred to it as the 'crumbs' and claimed it contained two clauses he refused to accept: one of them would oblige him not to complain to the media, and the other said he had no rights to the race. The contract was worth only £3200 to his company. Hone admitted he was willing to sign it if it wasn't for the clauses.

It was common knowledge around the city that there was some antagonism between Hone and some City Councillors, who felt that he would want to take some personal credit for any success that the road race might achieve. One unnamed Councillor was quoted as saying: "It won't be the Martin Hone show."

Hone himself explained it was his sheer enthusiasm and energy that resulted in banging tables and upsetting a few people in the early years. He argued it was his company that developed the idea, that he had fought for 19 years to bring international racing to the streets of Birmingham, and now he felt he had been squeezed out.

A *Motor Sport* magazine article about the Birmingham Superprix published in 2002 summed it up perfectly: "The man you have to feel sorry for the most is Hone, whose baby was snatched away from him at birth."

Hone insisted the city had lost thousands of pounds and wasn't supporting West Midlands firms enough. He claimed he had far better deals set up to buy the race and to sell the television rights than those made later by the city. He disapproved of the fact that London firms got the contracts and rights to video film, catering, ticket selling and road race sponsorships. The City Council counter-argued as Road Race Committee Chairman, Majorie Brown, said many contracts had been signed with West Midlands-based firms, and that Martin Hone's company failed to meet the City Council's requirements in its tender for the sponsorship contract.

However, there was plenty of positive news as the ticket sales office at the Birmingham City Council opened on 28th April, reporting a 'phenomenal' response with more than 300 seats sold in the first few hours. Bookings had been pouring in from all over Britain, such that coach companies based in Wales and Scotland made arrangements to bring race fans to the event.

Just as Birmingham was first to introduce motor racing in the streets of mainland Britain, it was first in allowing sponsors to name certain corners and straights of the Birmingham Superprix circuit, to attract sponsorship.

The Birmingham City Council issued a press release on 18th July, announcing that it recognised the "diligent and patient work to establish street racing in Birmingham's city centre" by Councillor Peter Barwell.

The Road Race Sub-Committee, chaired by Councillor John Charlton, was unanimously determined to name a hill on the circuit after Peter Barwell, who actually first mooted the idea of the event to then Town Clerk 18 years earlier when he was a recently elected back-bench councillor.

There was still an omission, with no mention of Martin Hone and his efforts to bring motor racing to Birmingham.

Peter Barwell commented on what it felt like to become a name associated with the Birmingham Superprix circuit: "Sometimes it has felt like an uphill struggle. But I and my colleagues have always known this could, should and would work for the city and the people of Birmingham. I am delighted to have played a part in bringing the glamour of Monaco, Brands Hatch and other major racing circuits to this great City of Birmingham."

The City Council decided to stage a dress rehearsal one month before the race. It was the official course test for the Halfords Birmingham Superprix, to be held over the weekend of 24th and 25th August. Only four drivers with their cars were invited for the dress rehearsal. No F3000 cars were present as the organisers made sure that a F3000 team had the advantage of lapping around the track before the initial Birmingham Superprix. Those involved were: Tony Trimmer with his 5-litre 550bhp Formula 5000 Lola T332; Roger Orgee with his F2 Lyncar; Mike Wilds with a 5-litre Chevrolet Thundersaloons car, and John Brindley with his Ford Cosworth-engined Sierra XR4Ti.

The official track test was on Sunday 27th July. Many citizens of Birmingham were thrilled by the city's first spectacle of racing cars on roads normally restricted to 30mph, and gathered behind the trackside barriers soon after 7.30am, for 30 minutes, to catch fleeting glimpses of the four test cars flashing by. This enthusiasm not shared by some disgruntled residents, however, who had been jolted from sleep.

The first comment by former Formula One driver Tony Trimmer was: "This is really exciting. It is a true driver's circuit. I love it." Later, when he stepped out of his Lola, he said: "This is a circuit that is going to sort the men from the boys. It needs precision driving, is certainly going to be very hard on the brakes – much more impressive than I had ever hoped. It is terrific."

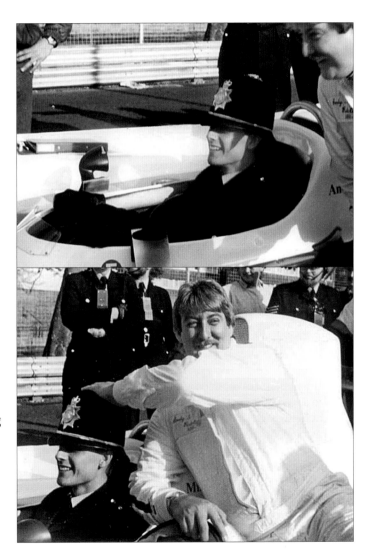

The police got into the spirit of things at the pre-race rehearsal.
(Jim Lamb)

1986: Tony Trimmer flies down Bristol Street, after the policemen had finished playing. (Jim Lamb)

Trimmer lapped around the 2.4 mile circuit with an average speed of 97mph (1 minute 40 seconds). It was thought the F3000 cars should be about 10 seconds, perhaps more, quicker than Trimmer's time because he had to slow down at sections that required cautious handling in places where the barriers had not yet been installed.

All of the drivers who took part in the half-hour long track test agreed that, in August, Birmingham could expect to see cars lapping the circuit at an average of 130mph, touching 185mph along Sherlock Street and Belgrave Middleway. Also, they generally agreed that the track surface was good and smooth, although ripples in braking points should make for some excitement.

The dress rehearsal was not just for the cars to test out the new street circuit. The track test was significant for the planning of emergency services by senior police, fire and ambulance personnel. The fire service took a video recording of the circuit, which would later be extensively studied by fire and police services.

Assistant Chief Fire Officer Rex Martin said a fire station would be maintained, and a number of other appliances strategically placed, within the circuit area. Assistant Chief Constable Paul Leopold said the track test would be fully assessed, and he felt there would be no reason for the first Birmingham Superprix to impose any problems for the police.

After the track test, the only change to the circuit requested by the drivers involved the removal of kerbs near an adverse camber at Highgate, which would be Halfords Corner. A week before the track rehearsal, the FISA and RAC MSA inspected and approved the street circuit, with only three minor changes needing to be made. As a display of the council's enthusiasm and eagerness to get things right, a hole had been cut in the wall of the wholesale market to provide a gravel run-off area!

1986 – The Halfords Birmingham Superprix

Sunday 24th August 1986:		
0900-1000	F3000	Untimed Group A practice session
1015-1115	F3000	Untimed Group B practice session
1130-1210	Thundersports	Heat 1 qualifying session: 20 mins untimed, 40 mins timed
1230-1310	Thundersports	Heat 2 qualifying session: 20 mins untimed, 40 mins timed
Lunch break		
1330-1400	F3000	Timed Group A first qualifying session
1430-1500	F3000	Timed Group B first qualifying session
1530-1600	F3000	Timed Group A second qualifying session
1630-1700	F3000	Timed Group B second qualifying session
1710 Race 1	Thundersports	Heat 1: 10 laps
1735 Race 2	Thundersports	Heat 2: 10 laps

Monday 25th August 1986:		
0900-0940	Pro-Am Renault	Practice session
1000-1020	F3000	Warm-up
1035-1100	FF1600	Qualifying session: 15 mins untimed, 25 mins timed
1120-1155	Formula Libre	Timed qualifying session
1100 Race 1	Pro-Am Renault	2x 5 laps
1300 Race 2	Thundersports	30 laps
1400	F3000	Warm-up
1435 Race 3	F3000	51 laps
1635 Race 4	FF1600	10 laps
1715 Race 5	Formula Libre	15 laps

Sunday 24th August 1986

Birmingham, on the summer Bank Holiday, 50,000 cars chasing 23,000 parking spaces, advance ticket sales of 40,000, 35 nations tuning in with a live television feed. The Superprix was set to put the city on the map. Locals tried anything to get extra free tickets, one asking for 28 – which he claimed were for mourners attending a funeral!

Things were not set to go smoothly, and it was discovered that vandals had interfered with the barriers overnight. Furthermore, some sections of the barriers had been incorrectly constructed and had to be altered. Due to the unusual anti-clockwise nature of the circuit, the Armco had been lapped over in the wrong way and the joints had to be changed over. The Armco joints needed to be in the direction of travel, the ending section on top of the new section, so there wouldn't be any problems if a car was to slide along it. Despite these

1986 programme cover.   Promotional leaflet.

'Street racing comes to Britain'
promotional folder.

difficulties, the proceedings got under way as planned, albeit two and three quarter hours late.

During the delays, the drivers became bored and the waiting crowd at the Bristol Street Straight were given a treat as the F3000 drivers and mechanics put on an impromptu display of football! Stuart Dent (Eliseo Salazar's British manager during the F3000 season) gave this story: "I played for Italy once! Well, sort of ... As was the norm in those days, a football was produced in the pit lane and some of the drivers started a kick-about. Then some mechanics joined in, and rolled out two pairs of trolley jacks as goal posts. The pits were in the Bristol

Street Motors forecourt facing a big grandstand, and the impromptu action was going down well with the bored and frustrated spectators.

"Within no time there were masses of players, and the goals had been made wider and the pitch lengthened. Such was the proliferation of our Italian friends in F3000 that season the players were split up to form Italy versus The Rest of the World.

"So, with the 'international' well under way, I was enjoying the action sitting on the barriers by the halfway line with Eliseo Salazar who didn't fancy a game.

"Then, out of the blue, the ball was propelled in

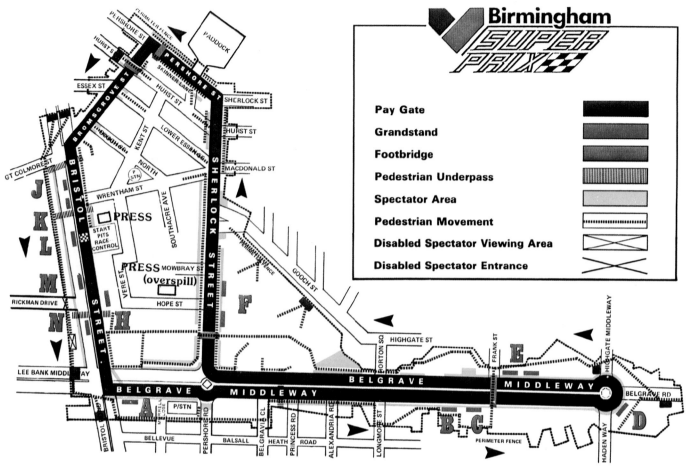

The Superprix circuit through the streets of Birmingam.

my direction ... Without a second thought, I sprung to my feet and hit the sweetest half-volley towards the goal mouth to my left. It was one of those weird slow-mo moments as everyone watched the ball's looping trajectory ... and saw it land plum in the goal – for the Italians!

"They went completely mad; Ivan Capelli and Gabriele Tarquini came rushing up to me and – in time-honoured soccer fashion – did all the embraces and stuff, and then turned me round to the grandstands, holding my arms up to the crowd (and those who weren't laughing too hard generously applauded!).

"It was just one of those brilliant and totally spontaneous moments – and, amazingly, Ivan still remembered it several years later. Oh what I'd give for a photo of those goal celebrations ..."

FISA later fined the race organisers £10,000 because of the delay.

An artist's impression of the first Superprix.

Finally at 11.45am, the unmistakable sound of an angry racing engine filled the air, John Nielsen in his Ralt-Honda rolled out of the pit lane; earning the honour of being the first driver to set a lap around the Birmingham Superprix circuit. The Dane clocked up a lap of 1m 24.27sec at an average speed of 105.5mph.

It finally had happened. After years of effort and disappointments, Birmingham got its race, and it was bound to be a great race for everyone to remember. Now, for the first time on the streets of mainland Britain, the people of Birmingham were witnessing high-powered Cosworth- and Honda-engined cars at race speeds. During that first session there were some incidents that caught the attention. Alain Ferté wrote off his March 86B after a manhole cover ripped through his monocoque and clouted a roundabout kerb. It happened when Ferté was making his debut

for the ORECA team and he had reason to be sour: "When my brake pedal went to the floor at the end of the straight, I just went straight on, but, unfortunately, there was a manhole cover there and it just ripped open the bottom of my monocoque ..." So he had to borrow his brother Michel's car for the duration of the practice session. The F3000 championship leader, Ivan Capelli, struggled with the car's setup and had to settle for only 9th.

Roberto Moreno received a scare in an unforgettable moment when he lost control of his Ralt, spinning across the run off area, out the other side, and through the open doors of the wholesale market! Thankfully, no-one was injured.

The Afamya Racing Shrike P15 goes past the Pershore Street multi-storey car park during a Thundersports qualifying session in 1986. (Robert Cairns)

A pair of spectators sneak a look out the window at the PC Automotive Royale RP40, driven by Richard Piper and Tony Trimmer during a bone-dry Thundersports qualifying session in 1986.

Martin Birrane trundles to a halt as his Tiga Cosworth's gear linkage snaps after one lap on the Sunday Thundersports qualifying session.

John Sheldon leans on his Tiga SC82 as he goes round

The PC Automotive Royale RP40 (driven by Richard Piper

Above: The John Williams/Phil Weaver March 76S tries hard to keep up with the more powerful Royale RP40 during the 1986 Thundersports qualifying session.

Above right: The nimble Royale RP37 (driven by Miles Berkeley and Anthony Reid) navigates Ferodo Corner.

Andrew Rickman's Class C Shrike P15, with the faster Class B Grange 85T driven by Jeff Wilson gaining some ground at the roundabout chicane.

Monday 25th August 1986

Race officials had mounted a night-long vigil to prevent the Armco barriers being tampered with and avoid a repeat of the vandalism that marred the qualifying/practice session and wasted so much time the previous day. The *Express & Star* quoted Andrew Marriott of CSS

David Leslie prepares for the start of the 1986 Celebrity Renault 5 race under wet conditions, ahead of local Birmingham MP Roger King. King was drawn in 5th place by ballot, using Peter Gottlieb's car.

Promotions: "Everything is set now and its all systems go for a memorable Superprix."

The timetable was modified once again:

0840	Thundersports	Heat 2 qualifying session
0900-0940	Pro-Am Renault	Practice session
1000-1020	F3000	Warm-up
1035-1100	FF1600	Qualifying session
1120-1155	Formula Libre	Timed qualifying session
1215 Race 1	Pro-Am Renault	2x 5 laps
1300 Race 2	Thundersports	30 laps
1435 Race 3	F3000	51 laps
1635 Race 4	FF1600	10 laps
1715 Race 5	Formula Libre	15 laps

Race 2: The Halfords Birmingham Superprix: 51 laps

As the crowd continued to grow around the street circuit, the rain became even heavier. Hurricane Charley had arrived, and it was a deluge! The cars set off on the warm-up lap, and into a ball of spray thrown up from the wet tyres. Visibility was poor and traction was worse. As a result, Tommy Bryne and Pierre Henri Raphanel had minor spins and, on arrival for the grid, Raphanel had to weave through to slot himself in the starting position at the fifth row. It was an offence that would end in disqualification.

At 2.35pm, the Halfords Birmingham Superprix was set to start. The tension built and, despite the weather, there was an electricity in the air. The cars were lined up, the warm-up lap complete, everything

Maurício Gugelmin enters the chicane with Ivan Capelli and Claudio Langes just coming out of the first corner of the street circuit.

was set – and ... nothing. The rain had drowned the electrics that controlled the start lights. The organisers frantically worked to fix the problem. The 'start delay' siren was set off and the Bristol Street Straight was quickly swarming with mechanics and organisers.

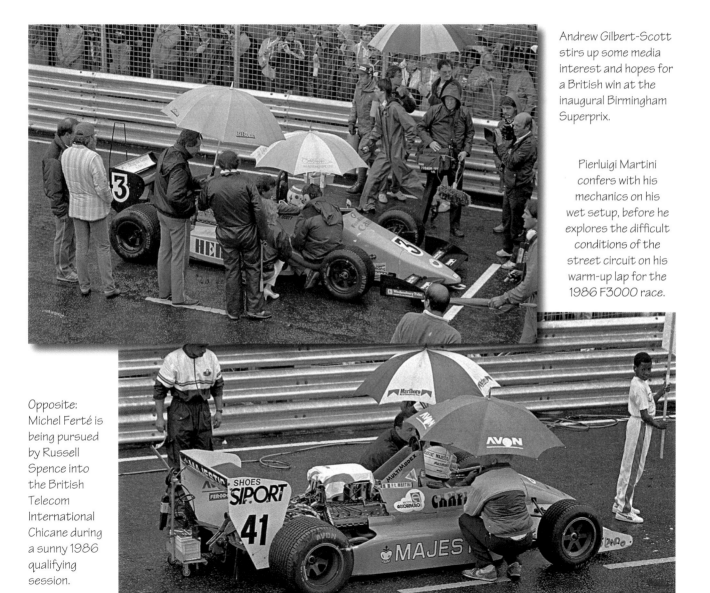

Andrew Gilbert-Scott stirs up some media interest and hopes for a British win at the inaugural Birmingham Superprix.

Pierluigi Martini confers with his mechanics on his wet setup, before he explores the difficult conditions of the street circuit on his warm-up lap for the 1986 F3000 race.

Opposite: Michel Ferté is being pursued by Russell Spence into the British Telecom International Chicane during a sunny 1986 qualifying session.

'Polesitter' Luis Perez Sala leads the field to line up on the grid and prepare for whatever the extremely wet race may bring.

Andrew Gilbert-Scott settles his Lola into its 2nd place position.

Eventually, after a 15 minute delay, the F3000 grid lined up again, ready for the race. With the start lights out of action the 'regridded' field was started in a traditional manner; John Nicol unfurled a union flag, and as he dropped it the F3000 cars were unleashed on the streets of Birmingham.

Pierluigi Martini smartly got off the line with Sala a safe distance behind him. Andrew Gilbert-Scott held on

to his third place, ahead of Michel Ferté. Eliseo Salazar couldn't see the flag, and most of the drivers had to listen to know when to start their race! Tommy Byrne described that first lap: "As anyone who was there that day knows, it was raining cats and dogs. I have never seen anything like it, but I was not too worried as I knew we could not race in those conditions, but I was wrong, and I never started so far back in any race never mind

Michel Ferté slowly pulls away ahead of Pascal Fabre, Eliseo Salazar and John Jones, after a Union Flag signalled the start of the first ever street circuit race in the United Kingdom.

the blinding rain. I was shitting myself and I had nothing to prove and I knew I was going to be injured; it was a given. There was no way we were going to get through the first turn without a major crash. I tried getting out of it, but I had to do it when the light went green, which I could not see from where I was. You could not see the steering wheel in front of you. I had to listen to the car in front to know when to brake for the first turn: when his engine died then I braked. It was a miracle that we all got through that turn."

It was indeed a miracle that, with the dangerous mixture of experienced and young drivers, plus dreadful weather conditions thrown in, the cars managed to get through the first turn and chicane with no problems.

There was a lot of standing water at the fabled Halfords Bump. Martini and Sala controlled their cars as best they could, but Gilbert-Scott went wide at the hairpin and Ferté, who was close behind, quickly overtook him at the Belgrave Middleway Straight.

Luis Pèrez Sala was clearly faster than his Pavesi team-mate, Pierluigi Martini, and pulled off an overtaking move for the lead at Tandon Turn. Gabriele Tarquini had the honour of being the first of many spinners. The next charger after Capelli was Eliseo Salazar. He was fast catching up on Andrew Gilbert-Scott, who was experiencing handling problems which resulted in a spin two laps later. Eventually, Salazar reeled him in.

There was a battle for second place between Michel Ferté and Pierluigi Martini. A big ball of spray was thrown up as they drove around the circuit, and onlookers thought the Frenchman would get in the front of Martini, though it wasn't to be.

Luis Pèrez Sala's lead was greatly reduced when he spun his car at the tricky Redex Bend on the tenth lap. His front nose cone was removed by the Armco but,

thankfully, he was able to continue with no damage to his front wings. At lap fifteen, he had to battle to survive being overtaken by his team-mate Martini, and Michel Ferté, as he started to experience wet and freezing feet!

The mishap cost Sala some five seconds, but what effect would the lack of bodywork have on his performance? Little, it seemed, for he continued to pull away from Martini and Ferté, leaving them to battle it out in the worsening weather.

The spectators were struggling to see the action in the heavy rain. Every now and then when something grey flew past in the spray they guessed it was a racing car, but couldn't be sure!

Famous (or should that be infamous?) commentator Brian Jones was providing live race commentary on the tannoy system, based in a shed on top of the portacabin at Bristol Street Motors. But the shed didn't have any windows and, somehow, the rain poured into the cramped commentator's booth. The only way Jones could tell what was happening in the race was by studying the sparks coming from the rear of the F3000 cars via a TV monitor.

On lap 22 the gap between Sala and Martini dropped to 3 seconds, but the leader was able to maintain his pace and his position.

At that point, people were beginning to wonder whether the decision might be taken to abandon the race. Everybody's worst fears about the dangerous conditions were confirmed when, as race leaders clocked up the 25th lap, Andrew Gilbert-Scott lost control of his car, on the exit of Bristol Street Motors Corner at a speed of 70 mph, on his 22nd lap. It could have been a harmless spin, but Alain Ferté's car was parked alongside the Armco and Gilbert-Scott's Lola smashed into the stationary March. The abandoned car was dislodged from its position, rolling across the entry of the BT International chicane, and the Lola faced the wrong direction (although correct for normal road cars!), littering the track with debris.

Andrew Gilbert-Scott escaped from the accident without injury, but he couldn't hide his disappointment: "The conditions were so bad you couldn't even see flag marshals or the light of the car in front of you ... although the grip of my car improved after I pitted, it simply got sideways coming out of the corner and I had nowhere to go. I don't think anything broke on my car, it just got away from me. It would have been a minor spin but for Ferte's car. As it was, I went in backwards and the engine of my car was knocked hard into the monocoque."

The cars that followed had to weave through the narrow gap left by the crash to get into the chicane. Marshals tried to push Ferté's car, but they struggled to do so.

To everyone's relief, the Clerk of the Course, John Nicol, decided to red flag the race. It was a very brave decision because of the hype the Birmingham Superprix was generating – in particular, the fact that the action was being broadcasted live to millions of viewers in 20 countries around the world. Some drivers felt it was necessary due to the appalling weather conditions, but some were disappointed not to have continued, to make up any ground they may have lost or didn't gain during the race.

For a while it was seemed as though the race would be run in two parts, with results decided by the total points from both races. Eventually, however, the decision was made not to continue the race for safety reasons and half points were awarded to the top six finishers, as had been done at the F3000 International Trophy Race at Silverstone earlier that year. Luis Pèrez Sala, who was

leading the race when it was stopped, was declared the winner of the first ever Birmingham Superprix. He commented: "I think the race should have been stopped earlier because the track got worse and worse every lap." Gilbert-Scott agreed: "These are the worst conditions I've ever been racing in, and I think it was very irresponsible to let us keep going."

Final positions after 24 laps:

1	Luis Pèrez Sala	42m 24.40sec (83.87mph average)	4.5 points
2	Pierluigi Martini	+2.31 seconds	3 points
3	Michel Ferté	+6.40 seconds	2 points
4	Eliseo Salazar	+11.65 seconds	1.5 points
5	Pascal Fabre	+42.99 seconds	1 point
6	Russell Spence	+54.84 seconds	0.5 points
Fastest lap: Eliseo Salazar 1m 42.62 (88.64mph average)			

Most of the supporting races were cancelled and the F3000 race cut short, due to the tight schedule of the timetable and the torrential conditions lashed out by Hurricane Charley. Luckily for the paying (and very soaked) crowd, they would be able to see some more racing action as the 'Pro' side of the Pro/Am Renault event was scheduled as the final race of the Birmingham Superprix.

Some drivers were angry and disappointed with the cancellation. FISA reinforced the point that F3000 cars got priority, and besides, there were television cameras to consider.

Amazingly, organisers never bothered to inform anyone about the cancellation of the Formula Libre, Thundersports and FF1600 races and competitors found out via an announcement from a local radio station. As a result of the race cancellations, some of the organisers helped themselves to the champagne they couldn't give away as prizes!

Marshals and organisers cleared away the debris and abandoned cars left behind from the previous race, but the weather wasn't letting up and many marshals had to seek shelter in the subways. According to Jim Lamb, who marshalled at the Formula Shell Corner: "a number of marshals learnt a valuable lesson about a good set of waterproofs at the weekend, as a number were treated for hypothermia, it was that wet!"

There was criticism from some national newspapers who viewed the Superprix as an anti-climax, more a consequence of the event's unique position in British motorsport than of any special dangers in the new street circuit. Monday's rainstorm was a freak incident and it was believed the Birmingham City Council, BRSCC and sponsors must wait for other years to reap the rewards of the Birmingham Superprix. It was, indeed, a cruel fate for a hurricane to hit Birmingham at that time, especially during the British summer.

It would require 12 months to put everything right and to address any issues; it would be foolhardy to think all of the problems originated from the appalling weather. On the day, it rained for a total of 14 hours! It made for the wettest ever F3000 race at the time, not an award that Birmingham would be proud of ...

The RAC MSA praised the organisers for their efforts, but there were lessons to be learnt – improving access points for the paying public and more provision of cranes to remove stricken cars from the danger points of the street circuit.

On Monday night, when the time came to dismantle the Superprix circuit and re-open the roads to conventional traffic, there was a moment of sadness behind the scenes. John Richardson, the Birmingham City Council's Divisional Engineer, said: "It is really soul destroying to see everything come down. We spend the weeks before the race transforming the roads into a race track and when it's finished you can stand there and not realise you're in a city."

Birmingham City Council would reflect upon the whole weekend. Its budget for the inaugural Birmingham Superprix was £1.5 million pounds and the event attracted 119,000 people over the Bank Holiday weekend (45,000 went to see the qualifying/practice sessions on Sunday). It estimated it would lose £400,000 but, in the end, the figure was actually £596,000. An estimated crowd of 70,000 attended on Monday.

John Charlton of the Birmingham Road Race Committee was quoted by the *Daily Mail:* "If the weather had gone with us, we might have been able to break even this year." *Motor* magazine also quoted him: "I'm satisfied that the city has achieved what it set out to."

History had been made, but there were still some lessons to be learnt. The world had seen that Birmingham could run a road race, even in appalling conditions. Now, the City of Birmingham hoped the weather gods would help it for the next August Bank Holiday in 1987 ...

1987 – The Halfords Birmingham Superprix street racing festival

Sunday 30th August 1987		
1000-1100	F3000	Untimed Group A practice session
1115-1215	F3000	Untimed Group A practice session
1245-1315	Modified Saloon	Qualifying session
1330-1400	F3000	Timed Group A first qualifying session
1430-1500	F3000	Timed Group A first qualifying session
1530-1600	F3000	Timed Group A second qualifying session
1630-1700	F3000	Timed Group B second qualifying session
1720 Race 1	Modified Saloon	10 laps

Monday 31st August 1987		
0900-0930	Ford Fiesta	Even numbered qualifying session
1000-1020	F3000	Warm-up
1045-1115	Ford Fiesta	Odd numbered qualifying session
1130-1200	FF1600	Qualifying session
1220 Race 2	Ford Fiesta	10 laps

Lunch break		
1430 Race 3	F3000	51 laps
1630 Race 4	FF1600	10 laps
1730 Race 5	Ford Fiesta	10 laps

The title sponsor of the Birmingham Superprix, Halfords, the automotive accessories retail chain based in the United Kingdom, confirmed a deal worth £750,000 for the next two years. Despite the 1986 Birmingham Superprix being spoiled by Hurricane Charley, Halfords regarded the event as a success, and decided to continue its support due to the huge amount of media exposure and publicity generated.

At the end of the tax year, after losses from the first Birmingham Superprix, the City Councilrevealed further losses of £173,051, although the total amount was topped with city sponsorship of £500,000. It was announced by John Charlton, Chairman of the Birmingham Road Race Sub-Committee, that the circuit would remain unmodified, but with more spectator facilities added after expectations of exceeding the spectator figure of 70,000 produced by the first ever Birmingham Superprix.

The F3000 circus arrived at the Birmingham Superprix for the second time, with hopes of a smooth and trouble free race. The cramped Bristol Street pits continued to be a problem, especially with the two-storey car park and its exit ramps, which made it difficult for teams to wheel their £75,000 cars in and out of the pits. It was laughable, but understandably infuriating for those concerned with the expensive machinery. History repeated itself however, as the first practice session was delayed by 90 minutes when it was discovered that dozens of bolts were missing from various sections of

Armco laid around the circuit. It was also unfortunate that the last of the 4500 lengths of Armco were not installed to the satisfaction of FIA circuit inspectors. A small problem with a gas main added to the delay. It was frustrating for the organisers, who had put in eight weeks of work to prepare and set up the Birmingham Superprix circuit, only to find these last minute problems. Thankfully, things were put right quickly and the first F3000 practice was able to start.

Jean-Pierre Frey pedals hard in his Team Dollop March 86B in an attempt to qualify for the 1987 Birmingham Superprix.

The low summer sun shines over the first race of the 1987 Birmingham Superprix, the Modified Saloon Race. A Class D Hillman Imp is sandwiched between Brian Chatfield's Rover Vitesse and Dave Brunsdon's BMW 2002Tii. (John Dean)

Robert Lee Lewis puts in his best F3000 qualifying effort, but it wasn't good enough to make the cut. Lamberto Leoni lurks behind in the fading sunlight.

A carnival atmosphere.

1987 programme cover and brochure.

Race 3: The Halfords Birmingham Superprix: 51 laps

Raceday arrived. The city of Birmingham was basking in lovely sunshine and there was a carnival atmosphere outside the street circuit. Organisers were expecting a good turnout, and 48,000 people came to watch the action.

The release of 100,000 balloons by the Bristol Motors showrooms signalled the start of the 1987 Birmingham Superprix. All of the 26 runners settled down nicely, amongst the basking sunshine which the crowd were enjoying at that moment. As the cars set off for their final formation lap, all but Roberto Moreno's left the grid, his works Ralt failing to fire up. Moreno put his

arms up in the air to warn the other drivers behind of his stationary Ralt. Four Husky marshals pushed the car off the gird and Ron Tauranac's mechanics worked to fix the car in the pit lane.

As the rest of the cars came around to line up, in front of the Bristol Street Motors showrooms, there was no need for a Union Flag to wave off the start of the race, the green lights came on without a problem!

Mauricio Gugelmin set off and laid some fresh rubber, but Stefano Modena and Andy Wallace made excellent starts and got ahead of the 'polesitter.'

Stefano Modena made the most of the clear road while the rest of the pack had to scrap for positions. Andy Wallace led the pack in 2nd, ahead of: Gugelmin; Grouillard; Tarquini; Trollé; Martini; Dalmas; Raphanel; Jones; Evans; Sala (he saved a fantastic slide at the bumpy Ferodo Corner); Andskär (up after a productive

Eventual winner Stefano Modena heads a tightly bunched group.

ahead of the chasing pack. Wallace then had to divert his attention from chasing Modena to defending himself against Gugelmin and a rapid Martini.

Wallace held off the onslaught from the Brazilian for a further seven laps, and Roberto Moreno gained a lot of ground up Peter Barwell Hill, into Halfords Corner. On the approach to Ferodo Corner, Wallace suddenly moved across and slid wide under heavy braking. His Madgwick Motorsport Lola careered over the gravel that covered a roundabout there, which it cleared before ending up in an escape road. He quickly booted the throttle and spun the car 180 degrees. When he rejoined the track he was in 5th, behind works Ralts of Moreno and Gugelmin, as well as Luis Pèrez Sala.

first lap); Barilla; Bailey; Euser; Hytten (after an amazing first lap); Leoni; Belmondo; Apicella; Foitek; Spence; Nurminen; Moreno; Langes and Ferté.

At the end of the sixth lap, Stefano Modena had built a good gap between himself and Andy Wallace, setting the fastest lap time so far of 1m 29.63sec, with an average speed of 99.2mph. Modena was even quicker on his next lap, setting a time of 1m 24.99sec (104.62mph). The Italian was in dominant form, increasing his lead to 8.5 seconds

City skyscrapers provide the backdrop as cars hurtle into Halfords Corner.

A packed grandstand thrills to a duel at Halfords Corner.

The Oreca Motorsport March of Olivier Grouillard shakes off an earlier clash of wheels with fellow Frenchman Pierre-Henri Raphanel's Marlboro-sponsored Onyx March at the start of the 1987 F3000 race.

Pierre-Henri Raphanel fends off Michel Trollé at the Pye chicane early in the 1987 Birmingham Superprix.

Maurício Gugelmin and Gabriele Tarquini get close at Ferodo Corner in pursuit of Andy Wallace's 2nd place at the 1987 Birmingham Superprix.

On the 16th lap of the 1987 F3000 race, Gabriele Tarquini loses 6th place to John Jones after his tachometer went wild, due to a misfire and an electrical fault in his First Racing March 87B.

Julian Bailey angles his Lola T87/50 into Ferodo Corner as a spectator stands very close to the action.

The crowd at Ferodo Corner couldn't believe what happened. Television viewers and onlookers gasped at the sight of Wallace blowing his 2nd position so close to the end of the race.

"He cost us six or seven seconds to Stefano (Modena)," moaned Moreno, "although I cannot say whether we would have caught him. Eventually, he got what he deserved, and I didn't touch him ..."

Stefano Modena was still well ahead of Moreno. The gap had increased when Wallace held up the Brazilians, Moreno and Gugelmin. He was running in a lonely race at the end. Moreno finally pulled away from Gugelmin who was struggling with a cracked exhaust; Gugelim had to conserve his car to make the finish.

Sinden goes off at Ferodo Corner during FF1600 qualifying. (Robert A Hollis)

Gary Evans gained 10th place with a brave move past John Jones.
The latter's team-mate and 1986 Superprix winner, Luis-Perez
Sala, is close behind. (John Dean)

Olivier Grouillard, Gabriele Tarquini and Michel Trollé jostle for position at the early stages of the F3000 race. (John Dean)

The sunny weather attracted more spectators, compared to the washed-out 1986 Superprix, as Stefano Modena pulls away from his pursuers. (John Dean)

Eventual 1987 Superprix winner Stefano Modena puts the hammer down along Metro Straight, more commonly known to local residents as Sherlock Street. (John Dean)

Above: Stefano Modena leads Andy Wallace into the Pye chicane at the early stages of the 1987 race.

Opposite, top right: Pierluigi Martini loses out to Maurício Gugelmin for 3rd place whilst suffering with a loose battery wire. You can also see Andy Wallace holding on to his 2nd place, ahead of the chasing duo.

Opposite, left: After his fuel pump failed on him before the warm-up lap, Roberto Moreno would start a stunning fight back from the bottom of the field to finish 2nd in the F3000 race.

Opposite, bottom right: A determined Andy Wallace going through his final laps of the 1987 Birmingham Superprix as he attempts to hold off a charging Roberto Moreno for 2nd place.

Modena led all the way to the chequered flag, a well deserved victory for the Italian. It was almost like a demonstration drive, except for his third gear jumping about over the bumps. About 11 seconds later, Moreno shook his fist in delight when he finished 2nd, some distance ahead of his team-mate and 'polesitter,' Gugelmin.

Final positions after 51 laps:

1	Stefano Modena	Winner
2	Roberto Moreno	+11.4 seconds
3	Mauricio Gugelmin	+13.2 seconds
4	Luis Pèrez Sala	+16.1 seconds
5	Andy Wallace	+32.7 seconds
6	Olivier Grouillard	+33.0 seconds
Fastest lap: Roberto Moreno 1m 22.91sec (107.24mph)		

After the problems at the first Birmingham Superprix, organisers could boast they provided non-stop excitement for the masses, particularly with the F3000 race, from the start to the finish. The only snag was a 90 minute delay on Sunday morning, but the street racing spectacular certainly made up for it.

It was a big disappointment for Wallace who said: "Everything was going well and I was able to run in second place for a large part of the race. Roberto Moreno was breathing down my neck in the works Ralt for a long time, but I was able to hold him off. Then my brake pedal got long (with wear – this circuit was very hard on brakes). Eventually, I arrived at the roundabout at the end of the second long straight and couldn't get

Justin Bell led the 1987 Formula Ford 1600 race on the first lap, from Gavin Wills and Derek Higgins, but threw it away when he crashed into the barriers. Higgins would go on to win the race. (John Dean)

Malcolm Holmes slides through the double apex of Ferodo Corner, with two similar Ford Fiestas in tow, during qualifying for the Ford Credit Fiesta Championship.

behalf of the RAC MSA's Hall, at the weekend. "Yes, we will be here next year," he said, as he revealed it would be the second showpiece for the Group A-based championship, situated right in the heart of the British motor industry. The Mod Saloon race featured some Group A cars – the prospect of Group A cars flying around the circuit would make people more excited.

According to the city council, it was revealed that 48 per cent of the crowd came from the rest of the country, with 48,000 people attending the F3000 qualifying sessions on the Sunday. There were estimates of 52,000 crowding into the 17 stands set up for the main event on Bank Holiday Monday. The event was also a success for local businesses, with a hotel survey concluding an 110 per cent increase in occupancy at that time.

Now, there was no doubt that Birmingham was here to stay and provide great racing. The drivers loved it, the spectators loved it and the sponsors loved it ...

the car stopped in time. I took a trip across the run-off and lost a couple of positions. A shame really, but in any case, a mistake on my part. I continued to finish 5th."

After a fantastic Bank Holiday with exciting racing all around, the BTCC organisers announced that the Birmingham Superprix circuit will host a round of the 1988 RAC British Touring Car Championship. It was announced by Series Coordinator Spence Hall, on

1988 – The Halfords Birmingham Superprix

Promotional leaflet.

1988 Superprix programme.

Promotional leaflet.

The Birmingham Superprix had been running for two years, and organisers felt it was time to up the ante and attract more spectators. With Birmingham being of such importance to the British motor industry, and with such a successful Formula Shell Modified Saloon race in 1987, more spectators were invited to the streets. Organisers also wanted to bring in an established racing saloon series, deciding to have a British Touring Car Championship race at the Birmingham Superprix. A little bit of history would be made, as the series had never before raced around a street circuit.

Race 4: The Halfords Birmingham Superprix: 51 laps

Following a very traumatic weekend at Brands Hatch, during which four drivers were injured, two of them seriously, the Birmingham Superprix missed two familiar faces. Michel Trollé broke several limbs at the fast Dingle Dell Corner during a needless free practice session, while Johnny Herbert joined Trollé in hospital after dislocating both of his ankles and breaking several bones in his feet – his career hanging in the balance after tangling with Gregor Foitek and causing a pile-up that wiped out eleven cars. Gregor Foitek escaped with a chipped bone in his wrist, and a black eye after being knocked out. It was suspected that Olivier Grouillard had broken his legs in the incident, though it transpired that he had extremely bruised ankles.

What would be learned from the carnage, and what would emerge at Birmingham the following weekend?

F3000 teams were aware of the balance sheets not looking too good so far into the season, especially after the Brands Hatch pile-up. People expected the teams and drivers to take a careful approach to the

Ferodo Corner during qualifying; clockwise from left to right:
Claudio Langes and Mark Blundell; Bertrand Gachot and Jari Nurminen follow closely; Michel Ferté, driving his Sport Auto Racing Lola, goes through the corner in confident style.

Birmingham Superprix, the unique street circuit with its notorious bumps, Armco surrounding the entire track, lack of run-off areas and tempting high speeds – so would they?

When the F3000 circus had finished fiddling and preparing its cars, twenty-six drivers set off for their warm-up lap at 2pm sharp. However, only twenty-five cars made it to the grid. The vivid green GDBA Lola of the 'polesitter,' Olivier Grouillard, was missing. A cruel fate, especially for the GDBA team after losing Michel Trollé, as a result of the Brands Hatch accident, and its racing budget being stretched to its coffers. It needed a

miracle and Grouillard had provided it. Though now, it was out of their hands.

The Lola's engine had died, and was suffering from electrical problems, too. Grouillard stepped out of the car and started running back to the pits, despite having sore ankles – a reminder of his 120mph accident in the eleven-car pile-up at Brands Hatch. He managed to get there as the cars starting from the pits were leaving for their warm-up. There was some hope he would be able to drive in the race after all. But it was all in vain ...

GDBA brought out its spare car which Olivier Grouillard's team frantically tried to start. There was a lot of commotion at the 'polesitter's' garage. Many Gallic oaths were muttered darkly while shoving and kicking to revive the spare car. It was such a tragedy for the stretched French team, which couldn't coax the car to life and now faced another engine problem. By then, GDBA mechanics were resigned to the fact that Grouillard wouldn't make it to the race. Eventually the pit lane was closed, and Grouillard's only hope now was to get out after the pack, exactly like Roberto Moreno when he stalled his car before the start of the 1987 race.

Pierre-Henri Raphanel took Grouillard's mantle to start the 1988 Birmingham Superprix. He was alone on the front row. The cars lined up carefully, although some front-runners strategically positioned theirs in a slight right-hand angle to get the best entry into the gentle curve of the Bristol Street Straight.

The F3000 grid started off smoothly, and only the 11th placed car of Cor Euser stalled for a very brief time; yellow flags were waved, but all of the cars avoided him and he pulled up to speed. Roberto Moreno suffered a lack of traction in his grid position and Pierluigi Martini went past Moreno for 2nd, shortly after the start/finish line.

The cars carefully funnelled into Molyslip Turn, with some of the mid-field cars braking hard. They all weaved through the difficult Pye Chicane and into Peter Barwell Hill. Some drivers had a good run up the hill, but eventually backed off before the opposite-camber Halfords Corner.

The fabled Halfords Corner bump was supposedly flattened, but all of the cars flew over it, providing an amazing view for the spectators in the surrounding grandstands.

Roberto Moreno got himself into the slipstream behind Pierluigi Martini and moved to the outside before the fast and bumpy Loctite Turn, where he got in front. It was a ballsy move, especially on the first lap of the race. He certainly knew how to drive to the maximum at the unique circuit, helped by his stunning comeback drive in the 1987 event.

Loctite Turn was very notorious for the sensitive F3000 cars. They tended to squirm and wobble on entering the difficult corner, but all of the front-runners went through with no major problems.

However, somewhere in the mid-field runners, Bertrand Gachot smelled blood on the first lap and went aside Claudio Langes before the Zenith Bend, while Andy Wallace was concentrating on making amends after his error at the closing stages of the 1987 race. Wallace entered turn 9 harmlessly when suddenly, and out of

The Gachot/Wallace accident at Zenith Bend. (Stuart Knibbs)

nowhere, Bertrand Gachot braked late and collided into him. Wallace's car spun backwards into the Armco and Bertrand Gachot's front nose went under the GEM Ralt. Wallace immediately raised his arms to protect himself in case the front nose of Gachot entered into his low cockpit. The rest of the mid-field and the back markers slowed to avoid the melee. Wallace recalls: "I was hit by Bertrand Gachot as I was turning in to one of the slow corners early in the race. It spun me around and put me out of the race. Bertrand was a bit of a crazy driver in those days. He simply missed his braking point, locked up, and slid into me. The stupid thing about all this was that it was very early in the race and that corner was not an overtaking spot as it was much too narrow. If you did manage to get inside someone there, you wouldn't make it through the corner without hitting the barrier on the exit. I have no idea what he was thinking. Not much probably!"

When the world-wide audience watched the first eleven cars come through Shell Turn, the last corner of the Birmingham Superprix street circuit, there was a big gap between the front-running cars and the mid-field cars. They must have wondered what the cause of the gap was, and then the inevitable happened ...

There would be chaos to occur further down the rest of the field. David Hunt experienced a difficult qualifying session but had made a smooth start and held his position at the back end of the F3000 grid. Exactly what happened next is not clear as there are various stories surrounding the event.

However, when David Hunt had driven along Sherlock Street Straight in his Roger Cowman Racing Lola at speeds of 120mph, he had qualified for his second race in succession. Now, he was unaware of the Wallace/Gachot melee ahead of him and the fact that

Claudio Langes had slowed down. Hunt's Lola reacted so badly on the bumpy surface of the braking zone at turn 8 that he lost control at high speed and the car spun sideways.

There was a high painted kerb and small gravel trap on the outside of the turn. At the other end of the gravel trap was a tyre wall, protecting a wholesaler's shop wall. The spinning Lola slid backwards and its rear jumped up in the air, aided by the high kerb. The gravel trap failed to stop the spinning Lola and the rear end of the car hurtled above the tyre wall. With ferocity and such high speed, the spinning Lola managed to punch a big hole in the wholesaler's shop wall.

The wall didn't absorb the deceleration of the Lola and after the impact the car rode alongside it very briefly, before it was thrown back onto the track. Hunt's car had disintegrated as the impact ripped the underfloor and tore the engine from the tub.

The Lola came to a rest upside down and, within a few seconds, about 20 marshals and fire crew had arrived at the scene of chaos. There was spilt fuel over the circuit and carbon fibre debris surrounded the mangled and unrecognisable Lola T88/50.

The marshals carefully righted the car to enable access for the medical crew. An ambulance arrived from nearby and the paramedics came to aid. Hunt was slumped in his cockpit, although from television footage he could be seen moving about, still strapped in the car.

At the same time, Bertrand Gachot's car limped from its collision with Andy Wallace into the pits, minus its entire front nose assembly. It was reported that, according to Gachot, Wallace was the one who had turned into him at Zenith Bend; he was trying to move behind Wallace but was hit by him, pushing Wallace's car into a spin.

Finally, the race organisers threw the red flag to stop the race. David Hunt's Lola was causing an obstruction and various people were working on the track.

Andy Wallace's Ralt was quickly winched away from the circuit with damage only to the front wings. Two medical cars exited the pits and had to drive around the whole circuit to get to the accident scene.

Mario Hytten, who was behind David Hunt's Lola at the time of the acident, recalls: "I was following David into Loctite Corner, and when I got on the brakes I thought I must have been miles too early, he just sailed away from me. Then I realised he was never going to make it. There is a big bump just before the braking area there. Perhaps his foot slipped or something. It happened to me a couple of times in qualifying.

"He was launched over a kerb, mounted the tyres and did a wall of death act. It was as though the car had been mounted there on purpose, really frightening. I thought for a moment he might land on top of me. When I found out that he was unhurt, I was amazed. I tell you, it was a big shunt."

The Fire Brigade mopped up the spilt fuel and oil with cement dust and the wrecked Lola was removed on two separate vehicles! The paying crowd was flocking towards the Loctite Turn to have a gander at the scene. The aftermath was broadcasted to television screens world-wide. The scene full of medical and fire crews, with accident investigators wandering around the crash site.

The investigators seemed to be pointing towards a certain position. Commentators pointed out that David Hunt had crashed into a wall, but that viewers weren't able to see the damage caused. A camera positioned at the outside of Loctite Turn, very near the gravel trap, then panned to its right to finally reveal the damage. It was, indeed, a "monster shunt" as described by David Hunt himself.

There was a massive hole in the wholesaler's shop wall, with stonemasonry debris all over the gravel trap and tyre wall. Large white scratches marked the wall where the gearbox of the white, Roger Cowan Racing, Lola had hammered into it. Marshals fixed the tyre wall. Bertrand Gachot's Spirit-TOM'S mechanics changed the front suspension and punctured rear tyres caused by a scrape with Claudio Langes.

The second start of the Halfords Birmingham Superprix

The Superprix race had initially started, after a considerable 90 minute delay, with 26 cars on the grid, but now there were just 22! Olivier Grouillard, Andy Wallace and David Hunt all out of the race, together with Pierre-Henri Raphanel who spun out with rear-suspension failure.

As the F3000 cars waited patiently for the lights to become green for the second time, Roberto Moreno and Pierluigi Martini began to inch forward very slightly. Then, eventually, the green lights came up and they shot off. Roberto Moreno struggled with lack of traction to get his Reynard ahead of Pierluigi Martini's March at the start.

Into the apex of the first corner, Cor Euser and Jean Alesi brushed very briefly, causing Cor to lock a wheel and smack into Volker Weidler's March. Weidler was spun around at the front of the pack, blocking the inside of the corner before coming to a standstill in line with the flow of traffic. The rest of the grid slowed down immediately in the melee, most drivers taking evasive action to prevent damaging their cars, especially at the start of the race.

The field divided into two groups around the Birmingham Superprix circuit. At the front, Roberto Moreno came out of the double apex, Ferodo Corner, quicker than front-runner Pierluigi Martini and went into his slipstream. Martini remembered how Moreno had overtaken him on the outside of Loctite Corner after the first start, and quickly moved across the track to take the inside line so Moreno couldn't take the lead.

There was much frustration amongst the second running pack to catch up with the front-runners. Eventually, at the Zenith Data Bend, Mark Blundell pulled off a brave move past Marco Apicella before the corner and took third place. Marco Apicella's March had better traction out of the corner and a chance to reclaim its position, but Blundell weaved to one side and then the other to block Apicella before they arrived at Shell Turn. Gareth Evans took his chance to nip past Russell Spence at the slow, first gear, Zenith Data Bend and nudged Spence into a spin.

The Reynard spun around, avoiding the Armco, and Gareth Evans went through the corner with no damage, but Russell Spence had other ideas ...

Spence's car blocked most of the track, and when Mario Hytten felt he could get through the narrowing gap and past the Reynard, Spence moved forward, closing the gap and causing Hytten to take evasive action by slamming on his anchors. Michel Ferté and Alfonso Garcia de Vinuesa followed suit, an opportunistic Ferté deciding to go around Spence instead, gently tripping over the Reynard's rear wheel before setting off. Marshals' were instructed to clear the driver and car safely, especially at such a narrow corner of the Birmingham Superprix circuit. However, Russell Spence refused to leave his car, putting his brakes on so the marshals couldn't safely remove it.

Mario Hytten and Alfonso Garcia de Vinuesa stalled their cars and began waving their arms frantically in the air. During the fracas, a traffic jam quickly built up amongst the mid-field and back-markers so one of the marshals decided to call for the crane to remove the stubborn Reynard. He promptly attached the car to the roll hoop and the whole farce was hoisted away five metres into the air. Russell Spence showed his displeasure with a display of colourful body language in the middle of the air!

Mario Hytten mentioned after the event: "That weekend everybody seemed intent on turning me into a pancake." When on the track he had a grandstand view of Russell Spence's undertray: "It did feel extremely precarious, and it felt very claustrophobic since my engine was now off. I was hemmed in by the car behind me and had no way of quickly extricating myself from the position."

Spence was quickly returned to earth where he chucked out his steering wheel and shouted at the crane driver. By now, the front-runners had finally made it around the circuit and were getting caught up in the traffic jam. There was no room for any of the drivers to manoeuvre their cars around the Zenith Data Corner. Cue red flag number two. As a result of this incident, Russell Spence and Alfonso Garcia du Vinuesa were fined $3000 for obstruction and failing to obey marshals' instructions. Spence was fined a further $500 for abusing the crane driver who lifted his Reynard away from the corner.

It was a big embarrassment that unfolded in front of the television cameras; it didn't show the sport in a slick and professional light, especially to the first time viewers/spectators. It was an extraordinary display of impatience from the mid-field.

The melee at Zenith Bend, which resulted in an irate Spence being removed from the track – still in his car! ...
(Stuart Knibbs)

... the cranes were busy that day. (Stuart Knibbs)

The third start of the Halfords Birmingham Superprix

An early restart was possible as the track had been quickly cleared, although the Onyx team protested that the half hour regulatory break should be enforced, providing it with a time window in which to fix Volker Weidler's March. The Reynards of Cor Euser and Gareth Evans were lightly modified and now ready to go. All of the initial 22 survivors were fit to take the third start of the Birmingham Superprix when ORECA frantically repaired Pierre Henri Raphanel's rear suspension, so

the car could be started from the pit lane. This increased the field to 23 runners!

The F3000 field lined up for the third start of the Birmingham Superprix; the number of laps had been reduced from 47 to 43.

Roberto Moreno had a trick up his sleeve for the start because he didn't want a repeat of the two sluggish getaways he'd already experienced. As the cars set up for the warm-up lap, he laid out some rubber in his grid position.

When the green lights came on, Moreno out-dragged Martini beautifully due to the rubber he had laid out on the track. Martin Donnelly, in his second ever F3000 race after his excellent debut win at Brands Hatch, made a stunning start and went around Pierluigi Martini on the outside of Molyslip Corner to grab second place.

Marco Apicella and Jean Alesi were close behind Martini, while Roberto Moreno stormed away from the whole grid. It was a very clean start for the F3000 runners, all aware that another delay would affect the outcome of the race and create more disappointment for spectators at the Birmingham Superprix.

Roberto Moreno continued his lead from a storming start, determined to strengthen his position. The other drivers were unable to respond and a big gap opened between him and the pursuing cars of Donnelly, Martini and Apicella.

After 10 laps, Moreno had increased the gap to 5 seconds ahead of Martin Donnelly, who was still well ahead of the First racing duo, Pierluigi Martini and Marco Apicella.

Martin Donnelly exits the Pye chicane with Jean-Denis Délétraz following closely. You can also see Olivier Grouillard's Lola, abandoned after it broke down on the reconnaissance lap.

On lap 24 there was a fright for the previously untroubled race leader when Fermin Velez spun his Lola directly into Moreno's path at the Zenith Data Bend. Moreno had to use all of his reflexes to avoid the stationary Lola at the blind corner. Donnelly gained three seconds from the incident, but Moreno quickly re-established the lost time a few laps afterwards.

Roberto Moreno had the race under control as he

put on his rev limiter and coolly counted down the laps. Donnelly was still well behind, unable to catch the slowing car of Moreno, despite clocking up the fastest lap of the race, two laps from the end, in a time of 1m 23.33sec and an average speed of 106.70mph. His lap was 0.01 seconds quicker than Moreno's fastest lap in the race.

Final positions after 43 laps:

1	Roberto Moreno	1h 00m 19.78s (105.02mph)
2	Martin Donnelly	1h 00m 27.48s
3	Pierluigi Martini	1h 00m 41.43s
4	Volker Weidler	1h 00m 57.48s
5	Bertrand Gachot	1h 00m 58.16s
DQ	Eric Bernard	1h 01m 08.30s
6	Michel Ferté	1h 01m 31.24s
Fastest lap: Martin Donnelly 1m 23.33s (106.70mph)		

Eric Bernard's excellent efforts, despite his mistake near the end of the race, awarded him the last points-paying position, with Michel Ferté in seventh. Some frantic efforts in the closing moments saw Jari Nurminen and Gareth Evans exchanging positions, with Nurminen having the final say on the last lap, before they capped off as the final unlapped runners of the day.

"The race was a special one, the race itself had to be restarted three times due to accidents, and the two first starts went greatly for us, the car worked like a dream, and I believed the car could have me up there in the top three," said the Finn. "After we picked up speed on the third start, presumably the tyres, which by then had been warmed up and cooled down three times,

didn't really work like they were supposed to, and that resulted in a very hard race overall."

All in all, it took three starts to get the race going and, almost unbelievably, the last F3000 races at Monza, Enna Pergusa, Brands Hatch, and now Birmingham, featured no fewer than 10 starts!

Minutes after the race, it was reported that a donkey had strayed on the circuit! 'Cecil the donkey' from the Cotswolds, due to star in *Joseph and the Amazing Technicolour Dreamcoat*, had somehow got onto the circuit, although the owner managed to coax him off soon afterwards.

Immediately, questions started to be asked about the planning of the whole event. RAC Coordinator Spencer Hall knew there would be problems, especially after the second start of the F3000 race and the event then running two hours behind the allocated schedule. Many people thought the organisers of the Birmingham Superprix would have learnt their lessons since Hurricane Charley wiped out the supporting programme.

Some stories of legal action against the organisers began to spring up and many drivers and team-managers made their feelings clear:

Phil Dowsett: "This bunch of FIA prima donnas should have their own events to play with where they don't have anybody else to screw up."

Dave Richards, team manager of the Prodrive BMWs explained: "We're absolutely furious about it. I can accept there were some mitigating circumstances, there usually are on a street circuit where accidents will occur. However, the fact that a couple of ragtag and bobtail support races were run in the morning, when we should have been racing, was ridiculous. What was especially galling was the total lack of communication between the organisers and the competitors. The first

Bill Taylor battles to stay ahead of Chris Banks in the Loctite Porsche Class A&B race, both driving similar Porsche Carreras.

During the Class A&B Porsche race, John Morrison and Brian Robinson battle for Class B honours.

I knew of the cancellation was when a policeman told me there was a six o'clock curfew, after which the roads would be re-opened. The championship organiser, Spencer Hall, didn't tell us the news for a further hour, and, even then, we had to go and seek him out.

"Obviously our sponsors weren't pleased, with 150 guests being entertained in Birmingham. So, we are looking to sort out the matter with the RAC MSA. In the future, we won't accept being treated in such a way and I can't see us returning to race at Birmingham, which is sad. It is all very sad because the whole thing could have been avoided with a little of forethought."

Steve Soper had done his homework, as he was quoted: "it was the same story in 1986, when the Thundersports people lost out. Someone should remember what happened then, and not have a repeat like we've had here."

It should never have happened, and the organisers should have had the sufficient experience to expect and cope with these kinds of problems. What mattered for the organisers was what they could learn from it to ensure it would never happen again. If the organisers wanted to make the Birmingham Superprix a major race meeting then they should have put in a few races, rather than trying to cram six races and qualifying into two days as allowed by the Birmingham City Council Act.

Overall, the FISA was displeased with the organisation and lack of progress from Birmingham City Council in extending the bill from two days to possibly 3 or 4 days, finishing either on any Sunday throughout May to September, or any Bank Holiday Monday in May or August.

The City Council needed some flexibility in the bill to avoid a repeat of the chaotic 1988 Birmingham Superprix event. They needed to apply for revisions to the Parliamentary Bill, and got a deadline of 27th November.

As a result, the FISA decided not to issue a track licence for the F3000 International championship round in 1989. Organisers had to convince the RAC MSA with their case before it got passed over to the FISA.

It was announced that Birmingham City Council had made a £43,000 loss on the 1988 event, and that it continued to lose money on top of the 1986 event (£596,000 loss) and 1987 event (£522,000 loss) to a total of £1.16 million.

Sometime in the autumn, the City Council set up a telephone poll to test public awareness of the event outside the West Midland region. It showed that 47 per cent of those polled recognised Birmingham as the venue for the Superprix. This compared with 70-80 per cent recognising the venues for the long established FA Cup Final at the Wembley Stadium, TT Motorcycle racing around the Isle of Man and the Grand National events at Aintree. Although, only 37 per cent correctly identified the venue for the Commonwealth Games and 17 per cent for the British Grand Prix.

Later on in the year, Birmingham City Council announced plans to extend the street circuit to 3 miles for the 1990 Birmingham Superprix. The Council had worked hard to get more flexibility over the race dates and the track layout. The revised bill would permit new pit and paddock facilities to replace the cramped Bristol Street Motors site.

It showed that the City Council was confident of making it happen, with planning happening well in advance for FISA-sanctioned World Championship events in the future.

1989 – The Halfords Birmingham Superprix

Sunday 27th August 1989

300 marshals, 400 St John Ambulance volunteers and 20 doctors were made available to handle any incident that might occur on the circuit, with seven vehicle recovery cranes and several recovery trucks scattered around the course. Birmingham Accident Hospital was within half a mile of the circuit – the closest to any circuit in the world according to the Council – with access via a unique priority corridor. There were 300 police offcers on duty over the two days, the majority of those were special constables. Hotels based in the city centre brought in extra staff and accomodation to cope with the massive increase in bookings.

Everything seemed to have been very well organised, although it was a shame the organisers didn't plan their souvenir programme properly – Damon Hill was named as Gary Brabham! But that wasn't the only mistake: Mark Blundell's photo was labelled as Eric Bernard; Martin Donnelly had the temporary name of Damon Hill; and Gary Brabham took Eddie Irvine's name. Finally, photos of Eric Bernard and Eddie Irvine were captioned as Martin Donnelly and Mark Blundell!

The F3000 untimed practice session

Local resident Stuart Knibbs refected on his memories of the practice session: "My mate and I made a big banner on a white sheet for the race, it read 'The DAMS busters – EJRacing' and we painted a picture of Donnelly's car in the bottom right-hand corner. We came up with that

1989 programme and promotional leaflet.

after seeing the EJR cars swamp the DAMS cars off the grid at Brands the week before.

"We had the banner opposite Eddie Jordan's pit during practice and he saw it and came out and gave us a wave! We also met Jean Alesi outside Matthew Boulton College, following the press conference. He liked the banner. He also signed my copy of *Autosport* that I had with me."

BTCC

The Birmingham Superprix received a royal seal of approval when H.R.H Prince Edwards arrived and drove a £20,000 Ford Sierra Cosworth around the circuit. It was his first time at a motor race, and he was initially driven around the 2.47 mile circuit by Nicol, registering

Sideshows at the 1989 Birmingham Superprix. (Peter Gillott)

speeds of 120mph, before being invited to take the wheel himself.

The Prince pulled away from the pit area at Bristol Street and raced around the circuit, pushing the car at 105mph. Afterwards, Nicol said: "He was a good driver. When I took him round we drove at about 115 or 120mph, and when he drove he reached about 105mph. I don't think he was too worried about the speeds we were going. He said it was interesting to be able to go over the speed limit legitimately."

The Prince stepped out of the Ford Sierra once he had completed his lap to attend lunch with representatives and officials from the Birmingham City Council, before leaving for the National Exhibition Centre to launch the 1989 International Youth Skill Olympics.

Frank Sytner, a Nottinghamshire BMW dealer, enjoyed his laps here last year: "The atmosphere was staggeringly good and the enthusiasm fantastic. It's a simple circuit, but a lot of it is blind. It takes a while getting used to driving down tunnels of Armco barrier and some of the bumps are severe. They actually give us an advantage, the BMW is terrifc under braking, even on the worst sections."

In the touring car qualifying sessions, Laurence Bristow put down some good laps, and later commented: "I just love this circuit, you have to be incredibly accurate and I think smoother as a result of that. The slightest little error gets magnifed so much. And following someone like Tim is mind-blowing. You could not see daylight between his tyres and the Armco on the exits.

Perfect precision is what you need here. This place is so much fun," he chuckled. "If you spent less time laughing, you might go faster," observed his team-mate, Tim Harvey!

There was a parade of West Midlands built racing cars going around the circuit during the mid afternoon 45 minute break. It was a welcome return for the cars, some returning to the Midlands for the first time. Motorsport historian Duncan Rabagliati's research combined with the restoration work carried out by owners to ensure a fine line-up of cars. The parade consisted of Alexis, Emeryson, Kieft, Kincraft and Ensign models. Some historical motorcycles also took part in the parade. There were stories that the Birmingham Superprix circuit might host a round of the World Superbike Championship in the future, but never anything more to suggest it would actually happen.

Monday 28th August 1989

On the Bank Holiday morning, it was a tremendous relief that the sun shined down on the City of Birmingham. It was no more than the organisers deserved. The whole meeting had run superbly, and bang on schedule. By early morning, 80,000 spectators had come to watch four races.

Race 4: The Halfords Birmingham Superprix: 51 laps

As the clock pointed out 2.15pm, it signalled the start of the fourth Birmingham Superprix. The 25 F3000 cars were lined up, basking in glorious sunshine, with the Deputy Clerk of Course, Tony Whitehouse, stood at the front of Jean Alesi. He held a yellow flag in the air and pointed to the person who would trigger the starting lights. According to Whitehouse, he was allocated

this responsibility because he was tall enough to be able to jump over the Armco to safety just before the race commenced! Alesi and Apicella crept forwards with some others before the lights went green, and the sounds of the Mugens, Judds and Cosworths reverberated off the surrounding buildings at Bristol Street.

Alesi and Apicella made a clear getaway. Emanuele Naspetti profited from Donnelly's wheelspin to take 3rd place, with his team-mate, Andrea Chiesa, ahead of him. Donnelly found himself in 6th, behind Erik Comas, as a result.

Just when it seemed as though everyone would getaway safely, Thomas Danielsson clouted into Claudio Langes' rear left tyre, sending the front of his Reynard up in the air, clearly askew from the rest of the body. The car went down an escape road at high speed and into a three-layered tyre wall. The tyres instantly wrapped around the Swede's car. Only one corner of his Reynard survived the scary accident, and, importantly, he escaped injury.

On that first lap, Alesi was determined to establish an early lead, but Apicella responded, after pressure from Chiesa at the Halfords Corner.

The three front-runners made a considerable gap between each other and the rest of the field. Television viewers witnessed the lovely sight of F3000 cars jumping about along Sherlock Street with the sunshine reflecting off nose cones. It was going to be a long and difficult day under those weather conditions, especially for Donnelly who was already experiencing colossal understeer with a full fuel tank behind him.

At the end of the third lap, Alesi was really going for it, setting what would be the fastest lap time of the race with a 1m 23.03sec (107.09mph) – 12 hundredths adrift

Eddie Irvine, Eric Bernard and Philippe Gache dive into Sherlock Street as they exit Ferodo Corner during the early stages of the race.

of Roberto Moreno's lap record, on only his third tour of the circuit!

The television production company provided a delight for its viewers when it tuned into some onboard footage from Andrea Chiesa's helmet. It gave a valuable insight into the Birmingham Superprix, especially its narrow and bumpy nature. It was rather interesting to see Chiesa checking his mirrors at the exit of corners around the circuit. He was positioning his head into the apex of the corners, fighting hard over the myriad of bumps.

By the fifth lap, Alesi had a three seconds lead ahead of Apicella. The First Racing driver now seemed unable to respond to Alesi's strong start. Comas was trying to

Mark Blundell, in the Cadbury-sponsored Middlebridge Racing Reynard, on his way to a 5th place at the 1989 Birmingham Superprix, the lapped Franco Scapini behind him on Peter Barwell Hill.

find a way past the Q8 Reynard of Naspetti. He had to be patient, though, as it was still early on in the race.

After his initial five lap burst, Alesi took a further five laps to extend his advantage by another second. But, from nowhere, Apicella began taking tenths of a second off Alesi's lead, and he continued to do so as the race progressed.

With the halfway point of the headline event fast approaching, it was a cracking race with battles scattered throughout the grid. On successive laps, the gap between Apicella and Alesi dwindled like this: 3.03 seconds; 2.84; 2.62; 2.50; 2.57; 1.62. The battle was on!

Apicella matched Alesi's moves around the track, as he had promised he would before race. Apicella tried to apply extra pressure on the Frenchman, but he couldn't find the extra yards of pace needed to get past the yellow Camel car. The First Racing Reynard was getting

stronger, with Apicella more confident than before – never allowing the Frenchman a moment to relax or to getaway. He would keep up the pace, hoping that the long-time race leader would make a mistake. Marco described his plan: "My strategy was to try to beat him at the start. When he took the lead, I held back and looked after the tyres. When I put in an effort I could catch him quite comfortably, but getting past was a different thing. He was quicker on the straights and all I could do was try to worry him into a mistake."

Apicella was all over Alesi's gearbox, still keeping up his attack, but couldn't find a way past the EJR driver. Only 0.30 of a second separated them at the line, with just a handful of laps to go.

Alesi finally made a minor mistake, when he was slow out of Cavendish Finance Corner, and it allowed Apicella to edge even closer. But the final attack never

Two mini battles occur at Monroe Chicane: Eddie Irvine fighting off Philippe Gache; and Eric van de Poele duelling with a charging Mark Blundell.

came from Apicella, and Alesi drove to the chequered flag. It was an emphatic and crucial victory for him because he had turned down the chance to drive a Tyrrell Formula One car at the daunting Spa circuit in order to fight for an F3000 Championship win.

Final positions after 51 laps:

1	Jean Ales	71m 48.98s (105.34mph)
2	Marco Apicella	71m 49.12s
3	Martin Donnelly	72m 26.68s
4	Eric Bernard	72m 46.33s
5	Mark Blundell	73m 04.66s
6	Eddie Irvine	73m 40.66s
Fastest lap: Jean Alesi 1m 23.03s (107.09mph)		

Despite the killjoys and difficulties of the early Superprix years, there was no doubt that the fourth Halfords Birmingham Superprix was a huge success. The motor race bill was needed to extend the race by an extra day so that the achievements could be converted into a triumph of the future. The publicity of the close racing and successes should confirm Birmingham's position on the motorsport world map.

John Nicol said that motor racing experts had travelled from many European countries to see the main event, and he was pleased with how it went. He said: "We actually had all of the FISA officials dancing on the table tops last night at the Holiday Inn. Councillor John Charlton could not contain his happiness at a post-race press conference in the eighth floor at the Matthew Boulton College, with motorsport journalists reporting throughout the world. He held up a copy of a Birmingham local newspaper, the *Evening Mail* with the headline 'Brumm laps it up!' That says it all. We had the ultimate in success with the Superprix. People from the race business have said it was absolutely first class. People told me they thought in 10 years' time the course will be better than Monaco. They recognise the immense potential of this event. It was a fantastic day – we just could not have had a better race. It was a brilliant event and the Superprix was a superb race. We have undoubtedly had the most successful Superprix ever."

The event had proved to be problem-free for the police, without any arrests on Monday and just two on Sunday, according to Supt Martin Burton of West Midlands Police: "It was really outstanding. Yesterday was actually trouble-free – it was quite remarkable. The police have got a lot to celebrate as well as the City Council."

Praiseworthy words, indeed, for Birmingham City Council and other important people, leaving the future of the Birmingham Superprix looking brighter than before.

The 1989 Birmingham Superprix attracted the biggest crowd and organisers felt they had got it right this time. Charlton called for the opposition to the Act to be dropped: "If there's any justice in this world then we will get our bill and it will go through Parliament ... Anyone who said that the people of Birmingham don't support this event should have been with me on the winner's truck as it went around the circuit after the Superprix. In flats and maisonettes, crowds were leaning from the windows, waving and cheering in huge numbers."

But another set of numbers made for less encouraging reading: a total loss of £1,649,000 over the four years of the Birmingham Superprix. The event was losing money and the organisers needed to do something about it, fast ...

1990 – The Halfords Birmingham Superprix

1990 programme and promotional leaflet.

at established street circuits normally registered at 90mph, while at the Birmingham Superprix circuit the average speed of Jean Alesi's 1989 pole lap was just short of 110mph.

Monday 27th August 1990

Damon Hill's day got off to the worst start when he discovered his VW Golf GTi had been stolen from the NCP car park at New Street station. Not long before, the self-same vehicle was also taken from outside his home in Wandsworth! Surely, he would have carried a miserable mood into the track for his F3000 race. Hill was not the only disappointed person at the event, though. John Gee was an observer, working as part of a team of elevated marshals in the middle of the Belgrave Middleway dual carriageway. He recalls being supplied, through the wire fence, with tea (and nothing else!) by some 'interesting' young ladies from the flats near the mosque: "We gathered they were in the 'personal services' industry and were pretty hacked off that the race was not bringing in the expected increase in business!"

Dave Vass was also supplied with hot beverages by local women whilst stationed outside the NGK Chicane. There was a police station nearby that doubled as a marshals' toilet: "Which we frequented at regular intervals because these dear old ladies, who lived right by the track, kept bringing us out cups of tea! The locals loved the event and all the attention that came with it."

But there was serious business to attend to – the main event.

Race 4: The Halfords Birmingham Superprix: 51 laps

In Britian, there was a lot of hope for a British winner to

Sunday 26th August 1990

The Birmingham race was different. Watching a driver working his way around the 2.47 mile circuit left you in no doubt that he was at work. Cars buckled about on the bumpy nature of the circuit and helmets rattled everywhere. Monte Carlo may have had more blind corners and Pau trickier cambers, but at Birmingham a driver got shaken about like a rag doll. "This place is for boxers or masochists but not racing drivers," said one, while another driver swore that it was even bumpier than last year. The average speeds the Birmingham Superprix, and Gilbert-Scott had the most chance of making it happen.

The clock ticked towards the 2.15pm start time of the race, and the 26 car grid was one short – the Leyton House team still rushing to fix Favre's car – when the lights went green. Birmingham, known as the capital of accidents and restarts from previous F3000 races, lived up to its reputation by providing a first corner collision involving four cars.

Apicella converted his pole position and pulled away very effectively from Chiesa, van de Poele and Gilbert-Scott. The pack was further reduced after Belmondo had a sluggish start and his car was forced into a spin in the mid-field: "I thought it was Artzet at first, but Gounon later came to apologise ..."

The Frenchman spun around and Hill, who was heading towards the stricken Reynard, managed to stop in time, only to be collected by Giovanardi. The Italian, who was already out of shape going into the corner, rear-ended Hill's gearbox. Barbazza tangled with Artzet, but managed to get away. Montermini managed to avoid damaging his car when he stopped short of the melee, before he selected reverse to join the race and promptly stalled his Reynard.

The inside of Holts Corner was blocked, and red flags were brought out around the circuit.

When Marshals reached the accident scene the drivers had already abandoned their damaged cars and ran for the pits to jump into spare cars. The organisers were keen to get the race restarted as the crane operator lifted the bold Superpower Reynard, hovering precariously above the spectators at the inside of the first corner!

When the race resumed, van de Poele got his start spot on, storming past Chiesa and Gilbert-Scott, before going around Apicella on the outside to take the lead at the first corner. Gilbert-Scott tucked in behind Apicella, ahead of Chiesa. The GA Motorsport driver led everyone into the NGK Chicane, only for Proulx to have a huge brake-locking moment that put him within a paper's width of colliding into Barbazza.

On lap five, Gounon fell foul to Bartels and Barbazza when he was correcting a slide out of a corner. The order would remain static until Chaves produced the first retirement of the race on lap eight. The small Portuguese had lost third gear and found it extremely difficult to hold the gear lever with one hand and drive the car with the other. "I lost third gear," he explained. "I tried to hold it in and drive with one hand. But Birmingham is too bumpy to do that. I had to stop."

The leader, van de Poele, also lost third gear but still kept his strong pace, with Apicella following suit. "I was having to use fourth rather than third in some fairly time-consuming places," he explained later. "My third gear was starting to jump out and my brake pedal was long. I had a big moment at the hairpin on one lap when I lost the brakes. Marco was also running less wing than me and I knew there was no way I could do anything about him."

Gilbert-Scott was still trying hard to keep up with the pace of the leading duo, and fend off an improving Frentzen as well. The bright yellow Reynard of Frentzen was inching closer to Gilbert-Scott – and to the barriers, too! On this lap, Apicella created a 1.35 second gap ahead of van de Poele and another fastest lap time of 1m 22.93s (107.22mph). It would be the fastest lap of the race.

On lap thirteen, there was a mid-field scrap between Irvine, Artzet, Bartels, Barbazza, Gounon and Tamburini. Artzet and Bartels looked to be more committed around

The two Camel Eddie Jordan Racing cars, of Heinz-Harald Frentzen and Eddie Irvine, sandwich F3000 series leader Erik Comas at Halfords Corner, during the restart of the 1990 Birmingham Superprix.

the unforgiving circuit as they kept chase with Irvine. Again, Apicella extended the gap and was now 2.07 seconds ahead of the GA Motorsport car.

On lap 19, Apicella started to get worried because he was losing power as the engine temperature was going up. Then, suddenly, the water warning light in his cockpit started to blink. He promptly slowed down and began to cry in his helmet. This man's luck was appalling as this was a real chance for him to get his first

ever F3000 win: "Still now I have pain when I remember the warning water light blink on ... I have to say that in my career is not the only time I lose a race for mechanic failure." He rolled his Reynard very slowly and sensibly into the pits before bits of his Mugen engine were sprayed all over the circuit. Apicella parked the car in his pit box and was visibly disappointed. The mechanics inspected the car straightaway and one of them identified a problem with the left-hand side radiator.

Allan McNish negotiates the wide Halfords Corner in front of a bumper Bank Holiday crowd.

A Lola floor stay had punctured through the side of the Reynard and penetrated the radiator. It was a cruel fate for him, and with Comas struggling a deserved nine points would have opened the championship up. "It's obviously impossible for me to win a race," he shrugged. "I don't know if my luck will ever change." The Italian nearly made it to Formula 1 with the Japanese Dome outfit (details in *Unraced* by SS Collins), but his bad luck remained and Apicella only ever started one Grand Prix, for Jordan, where he crashed out before the first corner. Today he races sports cars.

Van de Poele was now leading the Halfords Birmingham Superprix. Before Apicella retired from the race van de Poele had simply been keeping the Reynard in sight. The car was clearly smoking from early on, and obviously getting worse. People were sure that van de Poele was just sitting back, waiting for it to go pop before striding away into the distance.

On the 25th lap, Frentzen had a moment at Ferodo, but managed to keep his momentum and get close into Gilbert-Scott for the exit of Halfords on lap 26. He jinxed past Gilbert-Scott at Ferodo Corner with a superb move around the outside for second. Frentzen then began to eat away at van de Poele's lead of 5.9 seconds after 26 laps. After setting a lap time that only Apicella had bettered, Frentzen reduced the gap to 3.36 seconds after 28 laps. He was pushing hard, just barely ahead of the mid-field scrap, feeling like he had a chance of winning, only to bin it at Dynaglaze Corner in the gravel trap. He jumped out of his car and shook his head in disappointment. "After Apicella went out I really thought I could win," he said later, "but the car was oversteering more and more for several laps." It was a shame for him, considering van de Poele's problems, but a more experienced driver would have bided his time. "The car felt a bit funny for a couple of laps, as thought the steering rack was bent or something. It just got away from me," sighed the German. "When I saw van de Poele just ahead. I really thought victory was possible." It was the third time he had managed to find the same gravel trap over the whole weekend.

On lap 33, van de Poele lapped Warwick and had a seven second lead over Gilbert-Scott. The gap between van de Poele and Barbazza shrank to 13.5 seconds when Barbazza clocked up a lap time that would be the second fastest of the race (1m 23.22s). With just 15 laps to go, surely he couldn't do the unthinkable ... Barbazza was then within 13 seconds of the race leader. If he could get past Irvine there would be the wonderful prospect of a Leyton House battling for a win.

On lap 37, he passed Irvine around the outside of Ferodo Corner, only to skate wide onto the dirt and allow Irvine to repass for fourth. "I was wise to him after that," recounted Eddie, "so for the next couple of laps I stayed in the middle of the road to keep him at bay. I seemed to have the legs down the straight, but I wanted to protect my interests into corners. Particularly as I was having enough trouble braking as it was."

Barbazza attempted to repeat his move on lap 38. This time, he was on the outside of Irvine at Ferodo Corner, which follows the fastest section of the track, in an attempt to sell a dummy around the outside before he switched back into the inside. The kink towards Ferodo Corner didn't offer much room for two cars, and just as the Italian went inside he was surprised by the Camel EJR car's early braking. The Crypton chassis was launched over Irvine's right rear tyre and immediately tore off the left front wheel.

The Leyton House car was pitched into the barrier on the right-hand side of the circuit, the right front tyre continuing high into the air before entering into a sickening series of rolls. Barbazza's car flew across the roundabout, its nose digging into the gravel trap, and was launched into the guardrail at the escape road before it began to cartwheel away, 150 metres from the initial impact.

As the car flipped over and over, the left front section of the roll bar was compressed, wiping out the whole left-hand side of the car and perforating the chassis. He had come dangerously close to clearing the rails that guarded a 30 feet drop to an underpass below. Barbazza immediately walked away from a crash scene that ressembled a light aircraft accident. Marshals and a BRSCC rescue van quickly attended. He signalled to the ambulance men that he was fine, although his helmet clearly wasn't as it had completely split down one side from the massive impact!

It was then Chiesa's turn to mount a charge as the Apomatox driver, Gilbert-Scott, was finding his car to be a real handful. Chiesa was really gunning for it, and clocked up his fastest lap of the race (1m 23.42s). On lap 40, Chiesa was close to the rear of Gilbert-Scott's Reynard when he went too hot into the exit of the NGK Chicane. His PSR Lola skimmed off the racing line, battling for grip, and Chiesa almost lost control after he brushed the Armco. Fortunately, he continued on as Irvine was still limping around the track, trying to get his car back to the pits to retire from the race for good.

Gilbert-Scott pulled away up the Peter Barwell Hill before he appeared to lose power, allowing Chiesa to catch up again. Finally, Chiesa overtook Gilbert-Scott on lap forty-one, at the same place where he had touched the barrier on the previous lap. Warwick (who was already lapped by van de Poele) overtook Gilbert-Scott as well.

The Apomatox car eventually slowed dramatically, due to a right rear puncture. A struggling pit stop on lap 42 robbed Gilbert-Scott of any points after a superb weekend. It was unfortunate for the British driver as he dropped to seventh, a lap down. "The car was really difficult right from the start," shrugged Andrew.

On the final lap, van de Poele was very comfortable with his 20 second lead and took his second F3000 street circuit win of the season, having already won at Pau. Artzet and Gounon were gradually getting closer to Chiesa, but it was too late to change the positions. Gounon put Artzet under pressure, completing his fastest lap, but Artzet responded by going a tenth of a second quicker (1m 23.68s).

That was the way they crossed the line, and 1.5 seconds separated second from fourth. Artzet had scored Apomatox's first ever F3000 points. The only other cars on the same lap as the winner were the Reynard mounted Giovanardi and Naspetti; in fifth and sixth, the latter scoring his first point of the year.

The very unlucky Gilbert-Scott was a lap down, with Warwick in an excellent eighth after driving an under-powered car to achieve his first F3000 finish. Montermini and Wendlinger followed, while Jones was two laps adrift after a stop for a punctured left rear tyre.

Montermini had looked good during the warm-up session until he crashed at Honda Turn in the closing minutes. He then struggled throughout the race, the car jumping out of third gear and spinning twice. He had to complete a five point turn in an attempt to rejoin the race after one of his spins at the first corner, almost collecting

Jones in the process. In addition, he was without brakes or mirrors!

Positions after 51 laps:

1	Eric van de Poele	Winner
2	Andrea Chiesa	+18.94 seconds
3	Didier Artzet	+19.66 seconds
4	Jean-Marc Gounon	+20.48 seconds
5	Fabrizio Giovanardi	+33.16 seconds
6	Emanuele Naspetti	+43.45 seconds
Fastest lap: Marco Apicella 1m 22.93s (107.22mph)		

Van de Poele repeated his doughnut displays of 1989 at the Halfords Corner; this time all the more special for him. The Halfords Birmingham Superprix had still not produced a British winner. Martin Donnelly's 2nd place at the 1988 race was the best the Brits could do in the streets of Birmingham.

With Birmingham applying for a World Sports Car Championship round for next year, this event could mark the last appearance of F3000 cars on the city streets. Barbazza's monster accident highlighted possible problems encountered with single-seater cars in a very demanding street circuit environment. Although no-one was hurt, the City Council would need to consider even more stringent safety measures to safeguard the Birmingham Superprix for the future.

Godfrey Hall runs ahead of Frank Sytner's works BMW. He was losing a bit of ground and Frank Sytner was gaining into him, with Jeff Allam in tow, in a frantic all-BMW battle in the 1990 BTCC race.

The end of the road race

Despite the event's growing reputation in the motorsport community, there was negative news on the future of the Superprix following its fifth running.

The Birmingham Superprix was estimated to have made a loss of £500,000, according to event organisers. Once again, in a repeat of the alleged 'creative accounting' from previous years, taxpayers were likely to fork up £600,000 to bolster the losses.

It was a big disappointment as attendance figures were estimated to be 60,000, compared with 80,000 from the previous year's race which lost £439,000, before estimated promotional benefits to Birmingham were added to give an on paper profit of £115,801. The Council contributed £600,000 to the profits on the grounds that it was good advertising for the City of Birmingham. Also, the Superprix didn't receive enough publicity, with minimal coverage in national broadsheet newspapers and almost none in the tabloids. Nearly all of the race coverage outside the West Midlands consisted of a live telecast of the event itself to 3 million ITV viewers on Sunday afternoon.

Race organisers pointed out that if attendance figures had matched last year's numbers, the financial results would have been similar. "The accounts from last year show about £115,000 plus. I would think it will be about the same this year," said Councillor Bill Turner (Labour Lodge Hill), Deputy Chairman of the Council's motor race working party.

Councillor Turner also admitted that the Council would use taxpayers' money to cover the losses as it had in previous years. But he remained confident that the Birmingham Superprix would continue into 1991, reinforcing the fact that the sole purpose of the event was to promote the image of Birmingham.

Three Labour MPs (Davis, Rooker and Short) attacked the organisers, citing the financial figures as creative accounting, in a decision to press ahead at Parliament for the event to be scrapped.

Davis claimed the event had made a loss of £1.6 million in the last five years. In the Labour Party's manifesto for the city it promised to stop using public money as funding, but Council leader Sir Richard Knowles said it was up to the City Councillors to decide what to do with the Birmingham Superprix.

Race organisers were still hopeful that the future was safe. Then FISA announced that that year's Superprix would be the last to be run under the two-day format, as the event could not continue unless it ran over three days.

On Tuesday 28th August, it was reported that BRSCC's John Nicol made a claim stating that the FISA had changed its mind about the format. Organisers had to wait till the end of the year to find out if their bid to host a sports car race would be successful.

Martin Brundle followed suit with his approval of plans for a sports car championship race around the streets of Birmingham. "Jaguars, Mercedes and all other cars racing around the streets of Birmingham would make a wonderful sight," said Brundle, guest of honour at the Birmingham Superprix. "A street circuit is very demanding for a driver, but can also be very rewarding," he added.

It would be a big task to undertake as the current bill, with its two-day format, was suitable for the F3000 cars. For a WSPC race, a three-day closure would be necessary, and that required a new bill.

With news of a sports car race in Birmingham warming up, Superprix organisers worked hard to convince the FISA to allow a round of the WSPC to take place the following year. They planned to offer more pit space after the FISA complained the pits based in Bristol Street were inadequate for F3000 and not large enough for bigger sports cars. The flow of the track would be changed to a clockwise direction, allowing the pits to be located in the more spacious market area on the other side. Councillor, Bill Turner said: "We are hoping to change the direction of the circuit. The market area is the main part of the track being considered as a pit area because Bristol Street is too small."

Meanwhile, Birmingham City Council had been doing its homework, creating a survey for 1100 residents and businessmen to voice their opinions about the Birmingham Superprix being held over two days at the end of October.

Personnel visited people who had homes and businesses located around the street circuit, and those found to be unavailable were given the opportunity to telephone the Council to air their views.

The results of the survey were eventually released in the first week of November. The study revealed that 67 per cent of both residents and business representatives were in favour of the Superprix continuing in its present two-day format.

Understandably, only 1 per cent of residents covered in the survey were oblivious to the running of the 1989 event, compared with 4 per cent of businesses. 62 per cent felt the F3000 race was good for bringing publicity and encouraging jobs; just 1 per cent less residents concurred.

Councillor Ken Barton (Chairman of the City's General Purposes Committee) said of the survey's findings: "Once again, the people most affected by the staging of the Superprix have pledged their support by voting 2:1 in favour. Therefore, the City Council will abide by this overwhelming support and press ahead with plans for a race in 1991 if suitable funding comes from outside sources."

As the Council collected the evidence of its findings, it arranged a meeting on 2nd October to discuss the future of the street racing event. The Conservatives, who had backed the road race since it started in 1986, were angry because the controlling Labour Councillors were 'financially mismanaging it.' They were also upset because Labour MPs had blocked a parliamentary bill earlier that year. They wanted to scrap the event altogether, and hoped for support from Labour left-wingers opposing the event.

In response, Labour moved to hand the race over to private organisers to put off Labour left-wingers, who were also opposed to subsidising the race, from voting to end it. It was a shock move for the Birmingham Superprix to be handed over to private organisers to stop it draining million of pounds from taxpayers. Critics claimed the race had lost £2 million in five years.

They felt the Superprix should be privately funded and the 'Sunset Clause' provoked so that the event could not be supported with public money. The Birmingham Superprix would become a franchise.

The Labour authority made a last minute deal with the left-wingers to put the event out to be franchised. Hours after the Council's decision for the race to be privately organised and funded, the first offer to organise a bid came from a Birmingham public relations company, Key Communications. It said that it would be happy to unite businesses in consortium to tender for the Superprix. The Council felt it needed a new approach if the city was to get the benefits of the Superprix.

More surprising news emerged when the very man who dreamed up the idea of the Birmingham Superprix came forward as the one to save the event from closure. Martin Hone revealed that he had offered a rescue package to salvage the race.

His company, International Festival Services, had held talks with Sir Richard Knowles as long ago as July to try and save the event. "I am very pleased that the private sector is going to have a chance to become involved.

"Sir Richard came to my office with the deputy Councillor, Ken Barton, and senior officials. I told them the event was going down the pan and they must have some private sector involvement." Hone said.

Thirteen other marketing agencies and event organisers had also shown an interest in taking over the Birmingham Superprix event, after advertisements seeking private finance and management had been up for only two days.

City Councillors were surprised by the level of interest and wanted to make a short list of applicants by the end of the month, giving the Superprix franchise to the highest bidder. "We expected some private entrepreneurs to be interested in taking over the Superprix but the response is greater than expected," explained a Council spokesman. "The status of the event is not generally appreciated in Birmingham," he added.

The City Council were hit with a further blow when long-time supporter and MP Roger King announced he would no longer be trying to get the two-day event turned into a four-day race programme. He did not believe the opposition to the event was as great as some made out, saying: "It is a strange and unique situation whereby we have a Labour Council who are advocating the event and trying to promote it, and Labour MPs who are vehemently against it and blocking the bill in Parliament."

A week after the stormy council meeting, the Birmingham Superprix was put up for sale with a £1 million price tag through Alan Pascoe Associates. The city brought in the firm to produce a professionally assessed figure that could be written into the accounts.

The cumulative loss of £1 million was almost exacted, counterbalanced by the estimated £1 million of income from media and press coverage. This brought more controversy, as Terry Davies described it as 'legal fiddle.' He said the Council had created an advantage from a mistake, rather than deliberately creating a loophole in the bill, made possible because it had accidentally left a piece in the bill; stating that one of the reasons for staging a road race was to promote tourism for the city. Roger King countered by explaining that it was valid under the circumstances, and that promoters were in favour of local government accounting practices, which they felt the people would better understand, but opposition insisted on commericial accounting.

Davies maintained that he was not against the road race, and certainly not against the Council spending taxpayers' money on leisure activities. He felt the Council should set its priorities and that the money could have been better spent on social services. "I do not criticise the Council for having made a loss. I want to make that very clear. They were confident the road race was going to make a profit and, so, it was worth a try. If you never try, you never get anywhere. My criticism is that they said if it made a loss after five years they would stop it and they are not honouring this agreement," said Davies.

He also claimed that, because the Birmingham

Superprix was broadcasted around the world, certain areas were smartened up while others were left; only the sides of the block of flats that faced the camera were painted, others did not get the same treatment. This, he says: "is like changing your tie but not your underpants."

On 10th October 1990, the FISA made the announcement that it was continuing with its waiver for the event, and that it had withdrawn an ultimatum requiring the improvement of the pit safety standards.

However, the FISA vetoed Birmingham's bid to host a WSPC event that year. The city remained confident that it would be granted a round of the F3000 championship when the 1991 F3000 programme was to be announced in December.

Relieved Councillors set up a meeting on the same day as the FISA announcement, to invite bids for private funding to stage the 1991 Birmingham Superprix. The accounts of the street event indicated it would cost about £1 million to erect the race circuit and cover other charges. They also revealed that the Superprix event had lost £2 million on the five events.

A city spokesman said that he understood a licence would be granted for the following year's event. FISA officials believed the extra days were still necessary to improve safety standards and Councillors waited to hear if it would impose fresh conditions.

On Friday 1st November, when the deadline to find a new bidder had passed, the controversial Birmingham Superprix looked dead. Ken Barton, Chairman of the Road Race Committee, admitted that a deadline for private firms to bid to stage the event had passed without offers.

The *Daily News* headline on Friday 30th November bore this title: 'THE END OF THE ROAD'

The Committee had hoped to meet to consider offers, but private firms that were interested had changed their minds. The revelation that the Birmingham Superprix had lost a total of £2 million represented a huge stumbling block for bidders.

Councillor Barton said: "The possibility of staging the Superprix in 1991 is extremely remote. Sadly, this possibility will please some killjoys and certain sections who cannot see the wisdom in staging an event that creates jobs, encourages investment in Birmingham and provides a feast of entertainment."

Ironically, arch-critic Councillor Alan Blumenthal opened the sealed envelope for formal tenders for the event and found it was empty. "I thought it was a hoot," he said.

Reg Hales, Conservative MP of Sutton Four Oaks, said: "The loss of this race is a tragedy for Birmingham. The Labour group did not give private firms enough time to prepare for this. We asked them two years ago to begin turning this over to the private sector."

Clare Short was still sticking to her guns: "I am not surprised it has died. It has lost money since it started." It looked very much as though she wouldn't have to worry about F3000 and other cars racing through her constituency any more. Opponents of the race, including residents living around the circuit, doubted that it would ever be held again.

The Road Race Committee then heard that United Leisure Services, the giant leisure corporation that runs the American Super Bowl, was hoping to go into partnership with the City Council to salvage the race. The consortium, headed by American-based event management company Ogden Allied Corporation, had recently set up its British HQ in Birmingham. One of its directors, Terry Rutter said: "The Superprix was of great interest to us and we decided to go for it ... But we were asked to guarantee all of the City Council's substantial costs. They wanted an event which has made substantial losses underwritten for them. After a lot of evaluation and several trips across the Atlantic, we decided this was not the way."

BRSCC's John Nicol commented: "Although I have heard nothing official about a pull out, I have been tipped off. I know the Council has been looking for the promotion to be done privately and that nobody has been forthcoming. I understand, also, that Halfords has decided not to renew its contract."

On Wednesday 5th December, the FISA had its World Motor Sport Council meeting and confirmed the F3000 and WSPC calendars. The usual circuits, such as Jerez, Brands Hatch, and Spa Francochamps, were to host a round of the 1991 F3000 season, with WSPC cars taking part at classic tracks like Suzuka, Silverstone and Le Mans. The name of Birmingham didn't feature in the two racing calendars at all: it had been dropped, together with Donington Park and Silverstone.

So, that was it; no 1991 Birmingham Superprix for the meantime.

It was very disappointing news which, when combined with the weak economic climate at the time, and Halfords not wanting to continue its sponsorship as it had between 1986 and 1990, led to the Race Committee's decision to put the Birmingham Superprix event on hold till 1992, on which all resources and attention would be focused.

Race PR man Mike Hawkins told *Motoring News* on Monday 10th December: "The Motor Race Committee has reluctantly decided there will be no Superprix in 1991. As you know, we approached the private sector and invited tenders for the race.

"The door had been kept open with FISA,"

continued Hawkins, "and we will make an approach to resurrect the race for 1992 with private backing. Basically, we have parliamentary permission to stage a race if we want to."

Barton said the Council would keep £1 million worth of equipment, including safety barriers and scaffolding used to make the circuit, in storage for a future race.

Even the opposition admitted that it was a great achievement to have staged a motorsport race in the streets of Birmingham, requiring a lot of effort from dedicated people.

In the meantime, the City Council was still keen to keep things happening in Birmingham, especially on the August Bank Holiday, and promised to hold a motoring festival – but no competitive races – on the traditional Superprix date. "The bolts and Armco ain't up for sale," Hawkins stressed. The city still had powers to close certain streets over the August Bank Holiday each year for motor racing.

However, with no race scheduled for 1991, things began to look bleaker for the future of the event. An article in the *Birmingham Evening Mail* on 19th April bore the headline: 'CITY LOOKS AGAIN AT SUPER PRIX.' It stated that Ken Barton, Chairman of the General Purposes Committee, had said he would like to make use of the tons of Armco crash barriers lying idle somewhere. He said these steel beams would cost Birmingham £120,000 annually in repayments of loans, until the year of 2006. However, he did not rule out the possibility of a future Birmingham Superprix.

Though, over the year, people slowly accepted that the Superprix would not return for the foreseeable future. It left the Council in a difficult position, needing to consider what to do with the safety equipment.

Originally, before the inaugural Birmingham Superprix, the City Council used £2.4 million of taxpayers' money to buy safety equipment such as Armco beams, catch fencing, tyre walls, and other items. Then it had to sell off the equipment to a Dudley-based company, Ashton Plant Hire Ltd, for just £45,000. The City Council had been looking for a way to off-load the equipment and promptly contacted John Ashton. The sale was agreed and 700 steel beams were taken by lorry to the Dudley-based compound. The Armco couldn't be used again for roadside barriers because, after being kept in a storage compound for years, its quality had deteriorated. Some quantities were bought over the years to use for the rail industry, factories and roadworks. The Birmingham Superprix sell-off would close to an amount of £5 million in taxpayers' money.

At the end of February 1992, Council workmen refurnished and covered 2600 Armco post holes, located in verges, footpaths and carriageways, laid around the former circuit with special bollards. It is amazing to think there was a total of 8 miles of steel barrier beams around the circuit. Today, 4500 Armco pieces are still sitting in disuse in a compound outside Dudley, paint peeling with age.

Two years after the demise of the Superprix, the City Council wanted to host the 1993 RAC Rally, a round of the World Championship. A proposal was put forward for the start and finish of the week-long rally to take place in Centenary Square. Another idea was that the street circuit could also be used for a high speed stage.

This would be very convenient for the organisers as some of the Armco and other equipment was still in place around the circuit or in storage. Also a good idea for motorsport fans, as it would attract those hopeful of seeing racing return to the streets of Birmingham.

But not everyone was in favour. Mrs Christine Gazey, a member of the former Motor Race Community Action Group which opposed the Birmingham Superprix, said: "We would definitely form our group again if this goes through." Mrs Gazey, whose home was located on the bumpy Sherlock Street along the route of the former street circuit, also said: "We had five years of nightmare with the Superprix, and we are not having it again." Another member of the same group, Mrs Maureen Allen, said: "They will bring back racing over my dead body. We suffered enough last time. We will start up the protest group again. We don't want to go through any more of that misery."

Despite the objectors, people were still fascinated by the only street circuit in mainland Britain. The city Council revealed that it was still receiving half-a-dozen letters every week requesting information and tickets for the Birmingham Superprix. A City Council spokeswoman said: "In the main, the fans wants to know details of the Superprix and the exact route of the race. They say they want to stand on the circuit and try to visualise what it might have been like on race weekend. We are happy to oblige. And to help them, Superprix hoardings have never been taken down and there are no plans to remove them." Eventually, though, the advertising hoardings were removed and there is no permanent reminder nowadays. The start/finish line is barely there on Bristol Street, outside the Ford showrooms.

Three words – 'The Super Prix' – are picked out in white, orange and mauve flowers on the verge opposite Monaco House. The flowers grew sparser by the year and the Birmingham Superprix ceased to exist ...

On the August Bank Holiday, Councillor Peter Barwell, Birmingham Lord Mayor, was at Cannon Hill to flag the competitors off as guest of honour at the start

Rush hour traffic clogs the roads along Peter Barwell Hill and Belgrave Middleway, under a bitterly cold winter sunrise. (David Page)

of the Birmingham to Weston Veteran Car Rally. He was also there to welcome them at the end of their journey.

A week later, an event organised by Martin Hone called the Coventry Shakespeare Run – a 65 mile run through the Warwickshire towns from Coventry to Stratford-upon-Avon – took place.

Bristol Street, and the other roads used for the street circuit, had become eerily silent since the last controversial, and noisy, Birmingham Superprix shuddered to a halt; the event condemned to a small, sometimes forgotten piece of Birmingham's history.

The Superprix remains a quiet memory for now, marred by politicians' petty squabbles, with those in power incapable of seeing the unarguable benefits that a revived Superprix would bring. Imagine a horde of GP2 Dallara's screaming down Belgrave Middleway, or the buzzing ranks of British F3, all no doubt supported by the hugely popular BTCC ...

Racing cars would exit Bromsgrove Street on the final corner of the street circuit. Notice the extended wall; it was moved back to accommodate a bigger run-off area for the cars to exit the corner into Bristol Street. (David Page)

Looking back along Bromsgrove Street, the Pershore Street multi-storey car park in the background was a popular place for spectators. On one occasion at the Superprix, a particular photographer lent over the top of the multi-storey, with his friend holding on to his feet, so he could get a 'good shot!' (David Page)

This is what's left of Halfords Corner, unused since the last Birmingham Superprix in 1990. (David Page)

The road got narrower at this point in the circuit, leaving racing cars battling for position along the Belgrave Middleway. (David Page)

It's hard to imagine that racing cars have actually raced along Sherlock Street. Top speed was vital for the drivers here. (David Page)

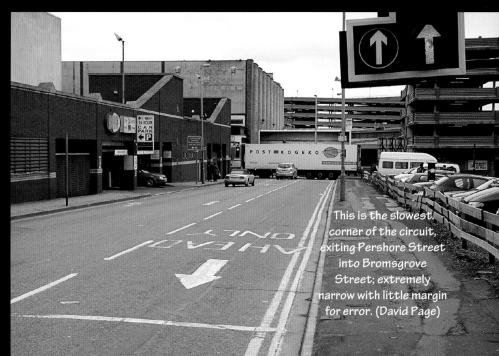

This is the slowest corner of the circuit, exiting Pershore Street into Bromsgrove Street; extremely narrow with little margin for error. (David Page)

The cars would power up along the bumpy Bromsgrove Street, after the slowest corner of the circuit. (David Page)

Approaching the gentle kink on the pit straight of Bristol Street, drivers would greet the sight of the chequered flag at the end of their races. (David Page)

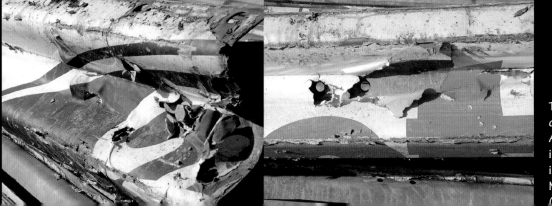

The remnants of the Superprix Armco lie rotting in a scrap yard in the West Midlands. (David Page)

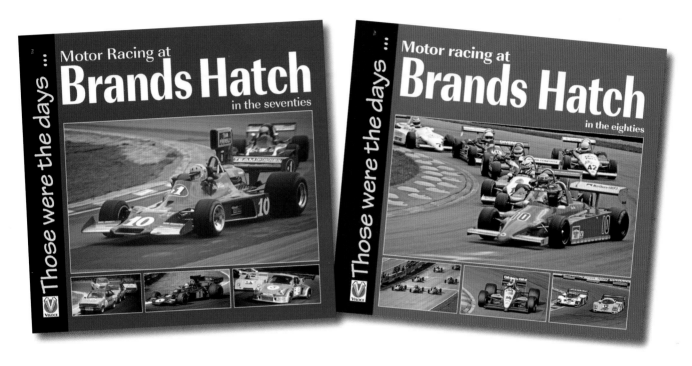

Two volumes covering Brands Hatch in its '70s and '80s heyday. Both feature many previously unpublished photographs, and offer a very personal account of visits to the world's busiest motor racing circuit during two decades of excitement and change, both on and off the track. An affectionate picture of motor racing at its very best, recreating the atmosphere at the track.

£12.99/£14.99
ISBN: 978-1-90478-806-5/ 978-1-84584-214-7

For more info on Veloce titles, visit our website at www.veloce.co.uk
email info@veloce.co.uk • tel: +44 (0)1305 260068 • prices subject to change • p+p extra

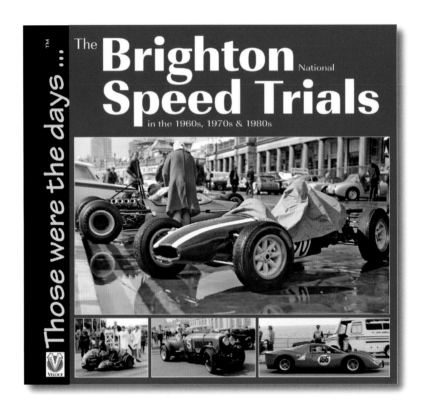

An evocative look back at the unique Brighton Speed Trials, first run in 1905. Captures the flavour and feel of one of Britain's oldest motor sports events. Over 150 previously unpublished photographs of cars and motorcycles chronicle the event from the '60s through to the mid-'80s.

£12.99
ISBN: 978-1-90370-688-6

For more info on Veloce titles, visit our website at www.veloce.co.uk
email info@veloce.co.uk • tel: +44 (0)1305 260068 • prices subject to change • p+p extra

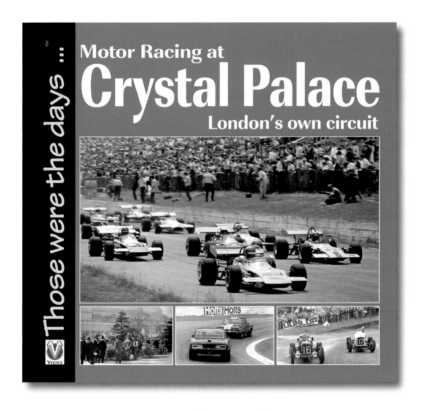

Crystal Palace, London's own circuit, has recently been identified as one of the oldest motor racing venues in the world – this is its story. Focussing on the development of the venue over the years and its untimely demise, many rare and previously unseen photos are included.

£12.99
ISBN: 978-1-904788-34-8

For more info on Veloce titles, visit our website at www.veloce.co.uk
email info@veloce.co.uk • tel: +44 (0)1305 260068 • prices subject to change • p+p extra

Index